Left **Portico of Pompey, Vaison-la-Romaine** Right **Provençal meadow**

Contents

Left **Marseille street scene** Right **St-Tropez**

As a guide to abbreviations in visitor information blocks: Adm = admission charge; DA = disabled access; D = dinner; L = lunch

3

PROVENCE'S TOP 10

10 Provence Highlights

Provence's top sights span the region's rich and varied history, from Roman arenas, isolated abbeys, and the palace of the medieval popes, to the more recent opulence of the belle époque era and the glamorous resorts beloved of the 20th-century jet set. Sunsoaked beaches, pretty villages nestled among lavender fields and a mountainous hinterland have inspired generations of artists, and continue to enchant every visitor to the area.

1 Palais des Papes
The honey-coloured walls and towers of this medieval palace, the seat of 14th-century pontiffs, dominate the delightful town of Avignon *(see pp8–9)*.

2 Grand Canyon du Verdon
The Verdon river flows through deep limestone gorges into the turquoise Lac de Ste-Croix, creating one of Provence's most stunning natural landscapes *(see pp10–11)*.

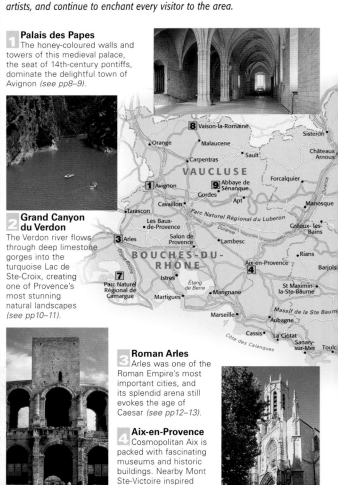

3 Roman Arles
Arles was one of the Roman Empire's most important cities, and its splendid arena still evokes the age of Caesar *(see pp12–13)*.

4 Aix-en-Provence
Cosmopolitan Aix is packed with fascinating museums and historic buildings. Nearby Mont Ste-Victoire inspired one of the greatest Provençal painters, Paul Cézanne *(see pp14–15)*.

Previous pages: **Pretty street in Nice**

7 The Camargue
Vast lagoons inhabited by wading flamingoes and plains with black bulls are just part of the protected landscape of the regional natural park of the Camargue *(see pp20–21)*.

5 Vieux Nice
Nice is a lively and sophisticated city, but its Old Town retains a quieter, authentic character *(see pp16–17)*.

8 Vaison-la-Romaine
A treasury of archaeological finds has been unearthed in this small town, once one of Provence's most important Roman sites *(see pp22–3)*.

9 Abbaye Notre-Dame de Sénanque
The great Cistercian abbey is a wonderful example of Romanesque religious architecture *(see pp24–5)*.

6 St-Tropez
Pretty and chic St-Tropez, with its yacht-filled harbour and gorgeous beaches, is the place to see and be seen on the Provençal coast *(see pp18–19)*.

10 Casino de Monte Carlo
Walk in the footsteps of princes, courtesans and film stars at the Riviera's most dazzling example of 19th-century grandeur *(see pp26–7)*.

TOP 10 Palais des Papes

In 1309, Pope Clement V transferred the papacy to France to escape political turmoil in Rome, and, for 68 years, Avignon became the religious, political and cultural centre of Christendom. The magnificent Papal Palace was built in just over 20 years, begun in 1335. Pope Benedict XII was responsible for the sober, Cistercian architecture of the Old Palace; his successor, Clement VI, added the New Palace in Gothic style, creating a massive ensemble of towers and stone walls soaring 50 m (165 ft) above the town centre. It remains a monument to the immense power of the papacy in the Middle Ages.

Fresco, St John's Chapel

🕖 Arrive early – the palace receives up to 4,000 visitors a day in summer.

The palace's excellent hand-held audio-guides are available in 11 languages (€2).

Ask for the Avignon Passion when buying your first ticket to any Avignon sight – it entitles you to discounts of 20–50 per cent on entrance to other sites.

- Place du Palais, Avignon
- Map B3, 04 90 27 50 00, www.palais-des-papes.com
- Open daily. 1–14 Mar: 9am–6:30pm; 15 Mar–30 Jun & 16 Sep–31 Oct: 9am–7pm; Jul & 1–15 Sep: 9am–8pm; Aug: 9am–9pm; Nov–Feb: 9:30am–5:45pm (guided tours in English Jul & Aug; phone for times)
- Adm €10.50 (€8.50 Nov–mid-Mar); under-8s free

Top 10 Features

1. Courtyard of Honour
2. Treasury Halls
3. Consistory Hall
4. St John's Chapel
5. Refectory
6. Benedict XII's Cloister
7. Pope's Chamber
8. Stag Room
9. Great Chapel
10. Great Audience Hall

Courtyard of Honour

The "meeting" of the two palaces is the best place to compare the respective styles. While the Old Palace resembles a defensive keep, the New Palace has finer stonework. Today the courtyard *(below)* is the venue for theatrical events during the Avignon Festival *(see p58)*.

Treasury Halls

The papal wealth was stashed beneath the flag-stoned floor of the Lower Treasury Hall. The Upper Treasury Hall was effectively the accounts department.

Consistory Hall

It was in the vast Salle du Consistoire *(above)* that the pope, cardinals and dignitaries gathered to consider key issues of the day. On the western wall now hang elegant 14th-century frescoes by Simone Martini.

St John's Chapel

Just off the Consistory Hall, this decorative gem was created by Matteo Giovanetti, a leading Sienese artist. The now faded frescoes depict the lives of St John the Baptist and St John the Evangelist with exceptional use of perspective across the walls and arched vault.

For more sights in Avignon See p122

Refectory

It was in the large refectory *(tinel)* that the pope entertained on feast days, such as a cardinal's appointment or a papal coronation. The pope would eat alone on a dais, while cardinals and guests were arranged around the room according to rank. The spectacular barrel-vaulted wooden ceiling was restored in the 1970s.

Pope's Chamber

The pope's bedroom gives a sense of everyday palace life. The pontiffs slept within blue walls decorated with vine and oak-leaf motifs.

Stag Room

Clement VI let his extravagant tastes run wild in his study. Frescoes cover all four walls, with scenes of hunting and fishing against a forest background – the most unusual decor in the palace.

Great Chapel

Of massive proportions, 52 m (170 ft) long, 15 m (50 ft) wide and 20 m (65 ft) high, with seven vaulted bays, the Grande Chapelle *(above)* was the scene of all kinds of religious celebrations, including papal coronations.

Great Audience Hall

This was the meeting place of the Court of Apostolic causes, the popes' forbidding judiciary against which no appeal was allowed. The hall's vaulted ceiling *(left)* bears a small remaining section of the Prophet's Fresco – unfortunately much of the fresco was hacked off and sold by soldiers during the palace's time as a barracks in the 19th century.

Benedict XII's Cloister

These four connecting buildings, surrounding a courtyard, date from 1340. Used for staff and guest accommodation, they were decorated by the Italian artist Simone Martini, who died in 1344 while working here. The Benedictine chapel is also part of the cloister.

Papal Avignon

The arrival of the papacy in Avignon brought great wealth and prestige to the town. When Pope Gregory XI took the papacy back to Rome in 1377 the French cardinals did not approve. On his death, they elected a French pope, while Italy elected an Italian one, putting the Christian world in schism. The row was resolved in 1417 and Avignon popes after Gregory XI have been considered anti-popes.

🔟 Grand Canyon du Verdon

The aptly-named Grand Canyon du Verdon is one of the most spectacular sights in France. Cutting deep into the rock, the Verdon river has created a series of gorges 25 km (15 miles) long and up to 700 m (2,300 ft) deep – a geography that prevented the area being fully explored until 1905. Vividly blue in places, foaming white where it storms through rapids beneath limestone cliffs, the Verdon flows south into the turquoise waters of the Lac de Ste-Croix, formed by damming the river close to Ste-Croix village. For the daring, the canyon offers rock climbing, whitewater rafting and hiking, while the 140-km (85-mile) drive around its magnificent landscapes takes a full day.

Notre-Dame-du-Roc, Castellane

🍴 Hotel-Restaurant la Provence (rte de la Maline, La Palud sur Verdon, 04 92 77 38 88) is a good lunch spot (Apr–Oct only). Specialities include jugged lamb with *herbes de Provence.*

🚣 From Apr–Sep, white-water raft trips are run down the canyon. Book with an operator in Castellane.

• Office du Tourisme, pl de l'Eglise, Moustiers-Ste-Marie; Map E3; 04 92 74 67 84; www.moustiers. eu; Open daily. Apr–Jun, Sep: 10am–noon, 2–6pm; Jul–Aug: 9:30am–7pm (9:30am–12:30pm, 2–7:30pm Sat & Sun); Mar, Oct–Nov: 10am–noon, 1:30–5:30pm; Dec–Feb: 10am–noon, 1:30–5pm
• Office du Tourisme, rue Nationale, Castellane; Map F3; 04 92 83 61 14; www.castellane.org; Open Sep–Jun: 9am–noon, 2–6pm Mon–Sat (May–Jun, Sep: 10am–1pm); Jul–Aug: 9am–7:30pm daily

Top 10 Sights

1. Route des Crêtes
2. Pointe Sublime
3. La Corniche Sublime
4. Martel Trail
5. Aiguines
6. Moustiers-Sainte-Marie
7. Lac de Ste-Croix
8. Trigance
9. La Palud sur Verdon
10. Castellane

1 Route des Crêtes

The Route des Crêtes requires a good head for heights and close attention to the road, but rewards visitors with unbeatable vertiginous views across the most spectacular reaches of the canyon *(above).*

2 Point Sublime

Close to the village of Rougon, Point Sublime *(right)* is one of the best places to look down into the rugged landscapes of the gorge. From here, the GR4 trail leads down into the canyon. Sturdy footwear is required, as is a torch (flashlight) to explore the tunnels cut into the cliffs.

3 La Corniche Sublime

The drive along the Corniche Sublime (D71), on the south side of the canyon, lives up to its name. Stop at the Balcons de la Mescale for a superb view and marvel at Europe's highest bridge, the Pont de l'Artuby.

4 Martel Trail
Forming part of the much longer GR4 walking trail through the canyon, the Martel Trail is the most popular hike through the gorges, passing dizzying cliffs and crossing narrow passes *(see p57)*.

5 Aiguines
A stately 17th-century chateau, with tiled roofs and white turrets *(above)*, overlooks this attractive village. There are panoramic views over the lake.

7 Lac de Ste-Croix
The hydroelectric dam which created this 10-km (6-mile) long lake south of Moustiers in 1974 generates much of Provence's power supply. Electric motorboats, canoes, windsurfing boards and catamarans *(below)* can be hired at Ste-Croix, Les Salles sur Verdon and Bauduen.

8 Trigance
This small, attractive village, with fine views of the rugged mountains which surround it, is a good place to stop for lunch on a motoring tour of the canyon.

9 La Palud sur Verdon
La Palud *(see p114)* is the base for organized walking expeditions into the canyon, whitewater rafting and kayaking on the rapids *(above)*.

10 Castellane
The pleasant, small town of Castellane is the largest community in the area and has the widest choice of places to stay and eat. Tour operators offer a range of activities in the canyon *(see p114)*.

6 Moustiers-Sainte-Marie
This lovely village *(right)* seems to grow out of the surrounding cliffs, with graceful stone bridges connecting houses on either side of the Ravine de Notre-Dame. Noted for its earthenware, it has a small museum and a 12th-century cliffside church, the Chapelle de Notre-Dame-de-Beauvoir *(see p112)*.

Roman Arles

One of the region's most charming old towns, Arles was originally founded by Greek traders but soon gained favour with Caesar and his successors and flourished into one of the most important provincial cities of the Roman Empire. Like many cities of the era, it was built to resemble a miniature version of Rome. Scattered around the narrow streets are relics of a lost empire, complete with the 4th-century remains of an emperor's palace, the remnants of a Roman circus and an arena where gladiatorial contests were staged, but all this gives only a hint of the town's wealth in Roman times.

Arles

⊘ **Save on entry fees with a "passport" from the tourist office.**

- Map B4
- *Les Arènes, rondpoint des Arènes; Open daily. Mar–Oct: 9am–6pm (to 7pm May–Sep); Nov–Feb: 10am–5pm; Closed 1 Jan, 1 May, 1 Nov, 25 Dec; Adm €6*
- *Musée Départemental Arles Antique, ave 1ère Division France Libre; Open 10am–6pm Wed–Mon; Closed as Les Arènes; Adm €8*
- *Thermes de Constantin, rue du Grand Prieuré; Open daily. Mar–Oct: 9am–noon, 2–6pm (to 7pm May–Sep); Nov–Feb: 10am–noon, 2–5pm; Closed as Les Arènes; Adm €3*
- *Les Alyscamps, ave des Alyscamps; Open daily. Mar–Oct: 9am–noon, 2–6pm (to 7pm May–Sep); Nov–Feb: 10am–noon, 2–5pm; Closed as Les Arènes; Adm €3.50*
- *Cryptoporticus du Forum, pl de la Republique; Open daily. Mar–Oct: 9am–noon, 2–6pm (7pm May–Sep); Nov–Feb: 10am–noon, 2–5pm. Adm €3.50*

Top 10 Sights

1. Les Arènes
2. Musée Départemental Arles Antique
3. Théâtre Antique
4. Porte de la Redoute and Tour des Mourgues
5. Thermes de Constantin
6. Les Alyscamps
7. Eglise St-Trophime
8. Egyptian Obelisk
9. Cryptoporticus du Forum
10. Place du Forum

Les Arènes
One of the most spectacular Roman relics in Provence, this well-preserved arena *(right)* has two floors of arches and seats for 12,000 spectators.

Musée Départemental Arles Antique
The finest collection of Roman sculpture in Provence. Highlights include a marble statue of Emperor Augustus, a statue of Venus and a massive Altar of Apollo.

Théâtre Antique
All that remains of the Roman theatre – once the hub of Arles – are these two graceful columns *(right)*, nicknamed the "two widows".

Porte de la Redoute and Tour des Mourgues
These battered gate towers stand either side of the former Via Aurelia, the highway which ran all the way from Arles to Rome.

Thermes de Constantin
A semi-circular apse marks the site of the once palatial bathhouse built in the 4th century, in the reign of Emperor Constantine.

7 Eglise St-Trophime

This spectacular Romanesque church, with its beautiful carved stonework *(left)*, was originally devoted to St Stephen. In the 10th century it became the church of St Trophimus *(see p32)*.

Roman Arles

9 Cryptoporticus du Forum

This amazing labyrinth of chambers *(below)* beneath the ancient Forum was the city's granary, carved out of the ground during the 1st century AD.

10 Place du Forum

Nothing remains today but the name of the Forum, the market which was the very heart of Roman Arles. However the place du Forum is still the hub of the town.

8 Egyptian Obelisk

The square-sided obelisk with carved features *(below)* is likely to have been a trophy from Rome's conquest of Egypt during Emperor Augustus's reign.

6 Les Alyscamps

An avenue of marble sarcophagi *(above)* marks the site of the Roman necropolis where the city's dignitaries were buried. Among the many legends surrounding the site, it is claimed that Christ appeared here.

Arles Bullfights

Les Arènes was originally built to stage the gory gladiator contests so loved by the Romans, and today is still the scene of battles between man and beast. During the bullfighting season, every seat in the arena is filled. Most contests are Provençal-style, in which the bull is not killed, but Spanish-style *corridas* also take place.

🔟 Aix-en-Provence

Aix-en-Provence is a sophisticated town. Whether in the dignified squares and little streets of the Old Quarter or amid the town houses and tree-lined avenues of the 17th- and 18th-century district, the atmosphere is self-consciously graceful. But it's also lively and fresh: fountains are ubiquitous, as are students at one of France's oldest universities; the calendar of artistic events is rich; and the markets are the best in the region. The Romans called the town "Aquae Sextius", which evolved into "Aix", after the thermal springs which continue to flow here. From the 12th to 15th centuries, the town was capital of independent Provence and established itself as a cultural centre, a reputation further enhanced in the 19th century by local artist Paul Cézanne (see p36).

Façade, Musée Granet

🔵 Aix's *calissons* are sweets made with almonds and fruit.

• Map C4
• Office du Tourisme, 2 pl Général-de-Gaulle; 04 42 16 11 61; www.aixen provencetourism.com
• Cathédrale St-Sauveur, 34 pl des Martyrs de la Résistance; Open 8am–noon, 2–6pm daily; Free (excl cloisters)
• Musée Granet, pl St-Jean-de-Malte; Open mid-Jun–mid-Oct: 9am–7pm daily (noon–11pm Thu); mid-Oct–mid-Jun: noon–6pm Thu–Sun; Closed 1 May; Adm €4
• Atelier Cézanne, ave Paul Cézanne; Open 10am–noon, 2–6pm (to 5pm Oct–Mar; 10am–6pm Jul, Aug); Closed 1–3 Jan, 1 May, 25 Dec, Sun Dec–Feb; Adm €5.50
• Pavillon de Vendôme, 32 rue Celony; Open 10am–6pm Wed–Mon (1:30–5pm mid-Oct–mid-Apr); Closed Jan; Adm €3
• Fondation Vasarely, 1 ave Marcel Pagnol; Open 10am–1pm, 2–6pm Tue–Sun; Adm €7

Top 10 Sights

1. Cours Mirabeau
2. Cathédrale St-Sauveur
3. Musée Granet
4. Atelier Cézanne
5. Rue Gaston-de-Saporta
6. Quartier Mazarin
7. Aix Market
8. Pavillon de Vendôme
9. Mont Sainte-Victoire
10. Fondation Vasarely

Cours Mirabeau
Created in 1650, Aix's majestic main avenue is a tunnel of greenery created by giant plane trees. In their shade stand elegant town houses and, on the northern side, smart, lively cafés. A succession of fountains adds freshness to the grandeur.

Cathédrale St-Sauveur
The focal point of medieval Aix (right). Notable features are the octagonal, 5th-century baptistry, the 12th-century cloisters and a wonderful Buisson Ardent triptych painted in 1476 by Nicholas Froment.

Musée Granet
Was built in 1671 as a priory by St Jean de Malte. Its exhibits include European art from the 16th to 19th centuries.

Atelier Cézanne
Cézanne's studio, from 1902 until his death, has been left as it was – a jumble of artist's paraphernalia, furniture and still-life subjects (left).

Rue Gaston-de-Saporta

Running from the town hall to the cathedral, is the liveliest thoroughfare of the Old Town, throbbing with commerce.

Quartier Mazarin

It was in this quiet district that the Aix nobility established some of their finest town houses in the 17th and 18th centuries. Within the tranquil sector of ornamental façades, small art galleries and charming antiques shops, the discreet, sober air of old money and aristocracy remains palpable.

Aix Market

The vast and colourful Aix market *(left)* colonizes all the town's old squares on Tuesday, Thursday and Saturday mornings. From the Place de Verdun via the Place des Prêcheurs to the Place de l'Hôtel de Ville, the streets come alive with stalls selling fresh produce, clothes and antiques.

Pavillon de Vendôme

Obliged to enter holy orders, local cardinal Louis de Mercoeur built this honey-stoned villa *(below)* as a love-nest for his mistress in 1665. Its size, decorated façade and extensive gardens, however, suggest a rather open secret. It now houses a collection of 18th-century paintings.

Mont Sainte-Victoire

To the east of Aix, this soaring mountain, 1,000 m (3,300 ft) high and 7 km (11 miles) across, exerts an almost mystical power over the region. Cézanne was so obsessed by its changing moods and intriguing shapes that he painted it more than 60 times. On the northern slopes is the Château de Vauvenargues, former home and burial place of artist Picasso *(see p36).*

Aix-en-Provence

Fondation Vasarely

This intriguing centre *(above)* is dedicated to Hungarian artist Victor Vasarely's work on the integration of art into architecture. Behind the geometric façade are displays of weird dimensions and perspectives.

Exploring Aix

Start at the Office du Tourisme, opposite the Rotonde fountain on place Général-de-Gaulle. If you want to follow in Cézanne's footsteps pick up the walking tour leaflet here. Otherwise, stroll up Cours Mirabeau to No. 55 (Cézanne's grandfather's hat shop, now a linen shop) and slip into the Old Town through the tiny Passage Agard. Return for a drink at the Café des Deux Garçons at No. 53 Cours Mirabeau, where Cézanne met other artists. Chic shops are in the Quartier Mazarin on the other side of the Cours.

Vieux Nice

Numerous foreign aristocrats and sundry rich and famous may have colonized other parts of the city, but Old Nice, just below the castle hill, belongs firmly to the Niçois, who claim it with Mediterranean gusto. Tiny streets throb with arm-waving commerce; Baroque architecture slots in among hanging washing, galleries, craft workshops and food stalls. The noise, aromas and colour recall the city's long links with Italy – Nice became French as late as 1860. The atmosphere lasts well into the night in the many bars, restaurants and clubs.

Palais Lascaris
From the façade to the grand staircase and 17th-century noble's apartments beyond, the scale and decor of this Baroque palace *(above)* is sumptuous.

Façade, Palais Lascaris

🔵 Resist free drinks on cours Saleya; they're offered by restaurateurs trying to tempt you to a table.

🟢 Vieux Nice is for pedestrians only. There's parking on place Masséna, blvd Jean-Jaurès and near cours Saleya and place Gautier.

- Office du Tourisme, 5 prom des Anglais, Map H4, 08 92 70 74 07 www.nicetourism.com
- Palais Lascaris, 15 rue Droite, Map H4, Open 10am–6pm Wed–Mon, Free
- Chapelle de la Miséricorde, cours Saleya, Open 2:30–5pm Tue, 10:30am Sun for mass
- Cathédrale Ste-Réparate, pl Rossetti, Map H4, Open 9am–noon, 2–6pm daily (but closed during mass), Free
- Opéra de Nice, 4-6 rue Saint-François de Paule, 04 92 17 40 00

Top 10 Sights

1. Cours Saleya
2. Palais Lascaris
3. Chapelle de la Miséricorde
4. Colline du Château
5. Cathédrale Ste-Réparate
6. Place St-François
7. Rue St-François-de-Paule
8. Quartier du Malonat
9. Rue Pairolière
10. Opéra de Nice

Cours Saleya
The great square (or rather, oblong) bursts to life in the morning sun every Tuesday to Sunday with the world-famous flower market. Come evening, bar and restaurant terraces buzz. On Monday mornings the flower market is replaced by an antiques market. This is Old Nice's focal point, colourful and vigorous.

Chapelle de la Miséricorde
If you see only one of Nice's Baroque churches, make sure it is this one. The splendour of the decoration makes it one of the world's best examples of the style.

Colline du Château
"Castle Hill" *(left)* was the stronghold of Nice until medieval times. The castle was destroyed in 1706, but the hill boasts breathtaking views.

For more on Nice See pp86–91

5 Cathédrale Ste-Réparate

When the Dukes of Savoy ruled Nice they worshipped in this soaring, 17th-century church, beneath the majestic dome and within the extravagance of the stuccoed Baroque decor.

Vieux Nice

6 Place St-François

This delightful square *(left)*, overseen by an 18th-century clocktower and a Baroque palace, is the site of the daily fish and herb market, held around the dolphin fountain.

9 Rue Pairolière

Here, street commerce reaches its zenith. Food shops spill over with *socca* (pancakes), salt cod and spicy meats, jostling for space amid Provençal frocks and jewellery. It's a bracing turmoil of aromas, colours and Niçois accents.

10 Opéra de Nice

This ornate building is home to ballet, classical music and opera. The theatre, designed by François Aune, a pupil of Gustave Eiffel, was reconstructed in 1885 following a fire which entirely destroyed the original. The opera house was classified a *monument historique* in 1993.

7 Rue St-François-de-Paule

This busy thoroughfare *(below)* is home to two Nice institutions: the Rococo, a sweetshop, at No. 7 and Alziari, olive and olive oil specialists, at No. 14.

8 Quartier du Malonat

Daily life courses through the tiny streets and squares, and beneath the washing and *trompe l'oeil* house decorations in the most authentic sector of Vieux Nice.

Baroque Churches

Vieux Nice is celebrated for its Baroque churches. In addition to those mentioned here, there are half a dozen others worth visiting: Ste Rita (rue de la Poissonnerie); Gésu (rue Droite), St Martin-St-Augustin (pl St-Augustin); St François-de-Paule (rue St-François-de-Paule), St-Suaire (rue St-Suaire) and the Chapelle des Pénitents Rouges (Rue Jules Gilly – Latin Mass every Sunday morning).

St-Tropez

Within the space of a short stroll it is easy to see why this sun-soaked, congenial fishing village, with its pretty harbour, red-tiled houses and fabulous sandy beaches, captured the heart of a generation of painters, Bohemians and later of holiday-makers. Despite all its hype as a world-famous tourism mecca of the rich and famous, "St-Trop" retains a good deal of its original charm – brightly painted fishing boats still moor in the Port de Pêche, although today they are increasingly outnumbered by gleaming yachts.

Notre Dame de l'Assomption tower

🄴 Le Café on place des Lices, formerly the Café des Arts, is where St-Trop's Bohemians hung out in the 1950s and 1960s heyday.

🄾 Visit the place des Lices on Tuesday or Saturday morning, when the square is crammed with gorgeous flower, fruit and antiques stalls.

• Map F5
• Office du Tourisme: quai Jean Jaurès; 08 92 68 48 28; Open daily. Jan–Mar, mid-Oct–Dec: 9:30am–12:30pm, 2–6pm; Apr–Jun, Sep–mid-Oct: 9:30am–12:30pm, 2–7pm; Jul, Aug: 9:30am–1:30pm, 3–7:30pm; www.ot-saint-tropez.com
• Notre Dame de l'Assomption: rue de l'Eglise; Open 9:30am–noon Tue–Sun; Free

Top 10 Sights

1. Place des Lices
2. Citadel
3. Vieux Port
4. Musée de l'Annonciade
5. Plages de Tahiti and Pampelonne
6. Notre Dame de l'Assomption
7. Tour Suffren
8. La Ponche
9. La Fontanette
10. Sentier des Douaniers

Place des Lices

This market square *(below)*, immortalized by the painter Charles Camoins *(see p35)*, still has some of the atmosphere captured in his work. Crowded with open-air cafés shaded by plane trees, it is the perfect place to watch locals playing *pétanque (see p78)*.

Citadel

The 17th-century ramparts surround a fort built to protect the village from Barbary corsairs. There are fine views of the village from the walls.

Vieux Port

The quayside of the Old Port, quai Jean Jaurès *(above)*, is lined with leisure vessels year-round. In summer the waterside buzzes with artists, and pedestrians hoping for a glimpse of someone famous.

Musée de l'Annonciade

Close to the Vieux Port, a pretty 16th-century chapel has been wonderfully converted to house a world-class collection of paintings by artists connected with St-Tropez, including Bonnard, Derain, Dufy, Matisse, Rouault and Signac *(see p34)*.

5 Plages de Tahiti and Pampelonne

St-Tropez's beaches begin 4 km (2.5 miles) south-east of the town, on the long bay called the Anse de Pampelonne *(see p42)*. The 9-km (5-mile) sweep of sand is divided into smaller stretches, each with its own name.

7 Tour Suffren

Built in AD 880 by Guillaume I, Duke of Provence, this round tower overlooking the harbour was once part of a larger castle, the Château Suffren. The tower overlooks the fishing harbour where old boats are moored.

8 La Ponche

La Ponche *(left)* is the core of the original fishing village. With narrow streets, painted shutters and ochre walls, it looks much as it did before tourism came along.

Artistic Mecca

How did St-Tropez transform itself from undiscovered fishing village to holiday hot-spot? Painter Paul Signac *(see p36)* must take half the blame: he arrived on his yacht in 1887, fell in love with the light and colour and decided to stay. Other painters followed, along with writers and would-be painters, attracted by warm weather and easy living. The film industry discovered the St-Trop scene in the 1950s, Brigitte Bardot became its ultimate symbol in the Swinging Sixties and the place has never looked back.

9 La Fontanette

The small La Fontanette beach, just east of La Ponche, is not as spectacular as those further afield, but is the only one within walking distance of town and ideal for a midday swim while exploring St-Tropez.

6 Notre Dame de l'Assomption

This ebullient Italian Baroque church built in the early 1800s contains a gilded bust *(right)* of the town's patron saint, Tropez (or Torpès). The Roman legionary converted to Christianity and was martyred by Emperor Nero, but he was pushed out to sea by the Romans and his body was washed up where the town now stands.

10 Sentier des Douaniers

The "Customs Officers' Path" is part of a *sentier littoral* (coastal path) with spectacular views of the coast. The tiny pebbly or sandy bays *(above)* offer bathing opportunities away from the crowds. The energetic can follow the path for 35 km (21 miles) to Cavalaire.

🔟 The Camargue

Black bulls, white horses and pink flamingoes: these are the classic images of the Camargue delta where the Rhône meets the sea and Europe's only cowboys gallop across the flattest land in France. It's a 800 sq km (300 sq miles) zone of lagoons, salt-flats and marshes; remote, romantic and rich in birdlife. Large stretches are protected and inaccessible, but open to all are the long evenings of gypsy music and wine as the sun sets on the horizon.

Camargue cowboy

🟢 For the real Camargue experience visit a *manade* (farm).

Mosquitoes can be a problem, so take insect repellent.

• Map A4
• Ginès Info Centre, Pont-de-Gau; Open Apr–Sep: daily; Oct–Mar: Sat–Thu
• Parc Ornithologique, Pont-de-Gau; Open daily (not 25 Dec); Adm €7.50
• Musée Camarguais, Mas du Pont de Rousty, 04 90 97 10 82; Open Wed–Mon; Closed 1 Jan, 1 May, 25 Dec; www.parc-camargue.fr; Adm €6
• Musée du Sel, Place Péchiney, Le Salin-de-Giraud; 04 42 86 70 20; Open Mar–Oct; Adm €8.20
• Parc Naturel Régional de Camargue, La Cape-lière; 04 90 97 00 97; Open Apr–Sep: daily; Oct–Mar: Wed–Mon; Adm €3
• Château d'Avignon, D570 10 km N of Saintes-Maries-de-la-Mer; Open Apr–Sep: Wed–Mon; Oct–Mar: Fri & last Sun of month; Closed 1 May, last week Dec; Adm €4

Top 10 Sights

1. Ginès Information Centre
2. Parc Ornithologique du Pont-de-Gau
3. Abbaye de St-Gilles
4. Musée Camarguais
5. Domaine de Méjanes
6. The Salt Pans
7. Plage de Beauduc
8. Les-Saintes-Maries-de-la-Mer
9. Parc Naturel Régional de Camargue
10. Château d'Avignon

1 Ginès Information Centre

A good place to start to understand the area's natural environment. Displays explain aspects such as dune vegetation *(below)* and a panoramic window looks over local birdlife in the wild.

2 Parc Ornithologique du Pont-de-Gau

Next door to the information centre is this splendid bird park. Aviaries dotted around two acres of marshland house birds that are difficult to spot in the wild.

3 Abbaye de St-Gilles

Located in St-Gilles-du-Gard, this once vast medieval abbey was severely damaged in 1562. The carved façade, the most beautiful in Provence, has survived intact.

4 Musée Camarguais

A converted sheep barn in Mas du Pont de Rousty is a fine setting for an excellent little museum dealing with the interaction of man and nature in the Camargue.

5 Domaine de Méjanes

On the banks of Vaccarès lagoon, tourist train trips travel through local flora and fauna and, on Sundays, there are bull-game spectaculars.

The Camargue

The Salt Pans

6 The largest salt pans in Europe *(above)*, in the southeast of the Camargue region, cover 100 sq km (40 sq miles) and produce 800,000 tonnes of salt a year. Reach the great mounds of salt by travelling on a little train from the Musée du Sel at Salin-de-Giraud.

Parc Naturel Régional de Camargue

9 The HQ of the Camargue National Nature Reserve of the Vaccarès lagoon and surrounding area is in La Capelière, and has well-presented information on eco-systems and climate. Nature trails and observation posts let you put your new knowledge to the test.

Château d'Avignon

10 Here's evidence that life isn't always a struggle in the Camargue. Surrounded by lovely grounds north of Les-Saintes-Maries-de-la-Mer, the chateau boasts the decoration of its 19th-century owners.

Plage de Beauduc

7 The beach at the end of the world. Its wild atmosphere has a hint of civilization, with the shacks and cabins having been pulled down.

Les-Saintes-Maries-de-la-Mer

8 The tiny main street and belltowers *(left)* of this old village seethe with crowds and colour in summer, but its seaside charm remains intact. The May gypsy pilgrimage marks the legendary arrival of Mary Magdalene, Mary Jacoby, Mary Salome and their servant Sara, patron saint of gypsies.

Camargue Bulls and Horses

The liveliest of the lithe Camargue bulls star in the *course Camarguaise* bull-running games, which take place in village arenas and on the streets. Camargue farmers also raise the larger fighting bulls for *corridas* in Spain and southern France. The Camargue horses which carry the *gardians* (cowboys) as they work only turn white as they reach adulthood. They are born almost black.

Vaison-la-Romaine

Vaison is a delightful town which is made all the more fascinating by its fine array of Roman relics, including a graceful single-arched bridge that miraculously survived the devastating floods of the Ouvèze River in 1992. The Romans named the town Vasio Vocontiorum and it flourished under their rule for four centuries, but with the collapse of the empire, Vaison was gradually buried by sand deposited by the flood-prone river. It was rebuilt in the Middle Ages, but it wasn't until 1907 that archaeologists began to rediscover the Roman city.

Théâtre Antique
The theatre *(above)* is a dazzling display of Roman building skill, with 34 semi-circular rows of stone benches ascending to a columned portico.

Remains, House with the Silver Bust

🔵 The modern area of Vaison is filled with numerous, chic pavement cafés.

🟢 Wear comfortable shoes, a sun hat and carry a bottle of water – especially in high summer.

• Map C2
• Office du Tourisme, pl du Chanoine Sautel; 04 90 36 02 11; www.vaison-ventoux-tourisme.com
• Roman ruins, Puymin and Musée Theo Desplans: pl du Chanoine, Sautel; Open daily. Mar, Oct: 10am–noon, 2–5:30pm; Apr, May: 9:30am–6pm; Jun–Sep: 9:30am–6:30pm; Nov, Dec, Feb 10am–noon, 2–5pm; Adm €8

Top 10 Sights

1. Puymin
2. Maison des Messii
3. Théâtre Antique
4. Nymphaeum
5. Portico of Pompey
6. Musée Theo Desplans
7. House with the Dolphin
8. House with the Silver Bust
9. Haute Ville and Pont Romain
10. Château

Puymin
This district *(below)* was the most important part of town in Roman times, containing the *praetorium* (court house), theatre, temples and shops. A broad road runs from the theatre to the main gate.

Maison des Messii
The House of the Messii must once have been the home of one of the town's most important families. Re-erected columns and foundations of an atrium, baths, temple to household gods, dining room and living rooms can still be seen.

Nymphaeum
The Nymphaeum was a rectangular sacred pool and fountain, covered by a roof supported by four columns. Traces of the building still remain, as does the sacred spring which provided the water supply. The area is now used as an open-air theatre.

For more Roman sights in Provence **See pp30–31**

5 Portico of Pompey

The impressive portico built by the family of Caesar's great rival Pompey is a massive, 65-m (210-ft) array of columns which originally surrounded an inner garden. Built around AD 20, it was demolished during the 5th century. Copies of statues *(right)* found on the site now stand in niches – the originals are preserved in the nearby museum.

8 House with the Silver Bust

Also named for a statue found here and now on show in the museum, the ruins of this once gracious villa, with its mosaic floors and paved hallway, are enhanced by copies of statues found here and elsewhere on the site.

9 Haute Ville and Pont Romain

Vaison's 2,000-year-old Roman bridge connects the upper town on the south bank with the north bank of the Ouvèze. The prettily restored old quarter *(below)*, with its 17th-century town houses, courtyards and fountains, is ringed by ramparts and entered through a massive, 14th-century stone gateway.

10 Château

At the highest point of the old town stands a dramatic, part-ruined castle *(left)*, built in 1160 by the Count of Toulouse. Three main wings and a formidable keep tower surround an inner courtyard.

6 Musée Théo Desplans

A muscular, life-size marble nude of the Emperor Hadrian, a statue of his empress Sabina, a gorgeous silver bust found at the Villasse site, and a six-seater public latrine are among the more interesting archaeological finds in this excellent museum.

7 House with the Dolphin

The House with the Dolphin was named after the marble statue of Cupid riding a dolphin which once stood here – it is now in the museum. The 2nd-century villa had a façade supported by 18 columns.

Abbaye Notre-Dame de Sénanque

Surrounded by the purple lavender fields of the Luberon, the grey stone façade of the lovely Abbaye Notre-Dame de Sénanque emanates tranquillity, but its past is anything but peaceful. Founded in 1148, Sénanque's golden age was the 13th century, when its ownership of several local farms brought new wealth. But in 1544 it was torched by the heretic Vaudois (see p118), in 1580 it was stricken by the plague, and by the 17th century only two monks were left in the crumbling building. The French Revolution and the anti-monastic laws of the 19th century were equally unkind, but since the 1970s, the abbey's fortunes have been restored, and ten monks are now in permanent residence here.

Dormitory, Abbaye Notre-Dame de Sénanque

➋ The most striking approach to Sénanque is from Gordes, with a perfect panorama of the abbey as the road descends into the craggy valley in which Sénanque stands.

- Map C3
- 04 90 72 05 86
- www.senanque.fr
- Open only for guided tours (in French). Reservation recommended. Phone to arrange. Closed mid-Nov–Jan (mornings), Ascension (sixth Sun after Easter), 15 Aug, 1 Nov
- Spiritual retreats (for a maximum 8 days) Feb–Dec; no arrivals on Mon. Phone or email frere. hotelier@senanque.fr to arrange.
- Mass given 8:30am Mon, 11:45am Tue–Sat, 10am Sun & bank hols
- Adm €7

Top 10 Features

1. Cloister
2. Spiritual Retreat
3. Nave and Transept
4. Apse
5. Dormitory
6. Calefactory
7. Tomb of Seigneur de Venasque
8. Chapterhouse
9. Channels
10. Lavender Fields

1 Cloister
The dove-grey limestone columns of the cloister *(below)*, decorated with delicate carvings of leaves, flowers and vines, are superb works of craftsmanship, dating from between 1180 and 1220.

2 Spiritual Retreat
Members of the public who wish to temporarily share the monks' lives of silent prayer and meditation are welcome to stay in the Abbey. Guests are invited to participate in the monastic community and activities.

3 Nave and Transept
The barrel-vaulted nave and aisles of Sénanque are five bays long, and three stone steps lead from the nave to the square crossing, with its eight-sided dome. One of four altars is original.

4 Apse
The three windows of the raised, semi-circular apse symbolize the Holy Trinity.

Dormitory

The monks' dormitory is a huge, vaulted space, paved with flagstones. Arched windows *(above)* at regular intervals along its walls and two large, circular windows at each end make the room pleasantly light and airy.

Tomb of the Seigneur de Venasque

In one corner of the east arm of the transept is the only non-Cistercian element of the church – a lovely Gothic tomb *(right)* marks the burial place of Geoffroy, the 13th-century Lord of Venasque and the abbey's former patron.

Channels

The Cistercians came to this plateau seeking isolation, and built their abbey next to the region's only river, the Senancole. They channelled the water to flow through and under the abbey, providing sanitation, and irrigation for the gardens.

Lavender Fields

The Abbaye Notre-Dame de Sénanque is surrounded by fields of lavender *(left)* which make a spectacular setting for the buildings in summer.

St Bernard and the Cistercians

With their complete lack of decoration or comfort, Provence's most outstanding Romanesque monasteries, Sénanque, Silvacane *(see p72)* and Le Thoronet *(see p77)*, reflect the austere ideals of the Cistercian order, founded in 1098 by St Bernard, abbot of Clairvaux. Rejecting the ostentatious luxury of the powerful Benedictine order, St Bernard advocated a rigorous and pure monastic life within simple, yet graceful and harmonious buildings.

Calefactory

The calefactory is symbolic of St Bernard's injunctions against luxury: this was the only heated room in the monastery, and it enabled monks to read and write without freezing.

Chapterhouse

The walls of the square chapterhouse, the abbey's assembly room, are lined with stone seats *(below)*. Here the monks sat each day to hear the abbot read a chapter from the Rule of St Benoît or a sermon from the Bible.

Casino de Monte Carlo

A magnificent belle époque extravaganza, Monte Carlo's Casino was built in 1863 by Charles Garnier, architect of the Paris opera house. With its commanding position and dazzling views of Monaco, it is impressive enough from the outside. But within it is truly dazzling: a veritable temple to luck, luxury and ostentatious self-indulgence, haunted by the phantoms of royal and aristocratic gamblers including the Prince of Wales (later King Edward VII), Grand Duke Nicholas of Russia, and many more. The stage of the Salle Garnier attracted artistic talents such as the great ballet choreographers, Diaghilev and Nijinsky. Modern slot machines and video poker screens look decidedly out of place amid these grand surroundings.

Façade, Casino de Monte Carlo

🗝 If you want to gamble, ignore the roulette wheel and head straight for the blackjack table. It's the only game where the odds, ever so slightly, favour the player, not the casino.

• Pl du Casino, Monte Carlo, Monaco
• Map H3
• 00 377 98 06 21 21
• www.casinomontecarlo.com
• Games rooms for viewing only: Open 9am–12:30pm daily; Adm €10; Games rooms for gambling: Open 2pm–late daily; Adm €10/free; Salle des Palmiers: Open Jul: 10am–late Sat, Sun; Aug: 10am–late daily; Free
• No admission under 18; passport or ID card required; jacket and tie required in private lounges, appropriate dress elsewhere

Top 10 Features

1. Atrium
2. Salle Garnier
3. Salon Blanc
4. Casino Café de Paris
5. Renaissance Hall
6. Salle Europe
7. Salles Privées
8. Salle des Palmiers
9. Jardins de Casino
10. Café de Paris

Atrium
Paved in marble, the vast entrance hall is surrounded by 28 Ionic columns. The atrium links the casino with the Salle Garnier, and its grandeur gives a hint of what awaits within.

Salle Garnier
Named after the architect, the concert hall *(below)* is lavishly turned out in red and gold, its walls adorned with frescoes and encrusted with bas-reliefs.

Salon Blanc
The wall painting in the White Room, *Graces of Florence*, depicts three muses said to represent 19th-century French courtesans, Cleo de Merode, Liane de Pougy and Otero.

Casino Café de Paris
Replacing the casino's smoking room, this up-to-the-minute games room is situated inside the Café de Paris. It features modern machines and tables, and is reminiscent of Las Vegas.

6 Salle Europe
The opulent Salle Europe, where roulette is again the featured game, is lit by eight huge chandeliers of glittering Bohemian crystal *(left)*.

7 Salles Privées
The Salle Médecin, Salle de l'Empire and Salle Touzet are the casino's private rooms. Behind closed doors the high rollers gather, in surroundings of gilded mahogany.

9 Jardins de Casino
Opposite the casino are the magnificent flower gardens, immaculate lawns and lily pools of the Casino Gardens *(above)*, sloping up towards Monaco's most exclusive shopping area *(see p99)*.

10 Café de Paris
King Edward VII was a regular customer to the *belle époque* café in front of the casino, first known as the Café Divan. In the 1930s, while retaining its original façade, it was transformed into an Art Deco triumph and was lovingly renovated again in 1988 *(see p102)*.

5 Renaissance Hall
This large room filled with roulette tables *(below)* is the main gaming room. Its *belle époque* finery imitates the high style of the Italian Renaissance.

8 Salle des Palmiers
In summer, gaming moves to the Salle des Palmiers, a contemporary building with fine views of the sea from its lovely bars and terraces.

The Man who Broke the Bank

Many visitors to the casino still follow the superstitious tradition of stroking the knee of the horse – part of an equestrian statue of Louis XIV – in the foyer of the Hôtel de Paris, to bring luck. Luckiest of all was Charles Wells, who, in 1891, raked in one million gold francs in a three-day winning streak, then won three million more on a second visit. The event inspired the song "The Man Who Broke the Bank at Monte Carlo". But his luck failed in the end, and on a third visit the casino cleaned him out.

Left **Ancient village huts, Gordes** Right **Roman mosaic, Vaison-la-Romaine**

🔟 Moments in History

1 Early Settlers
Carvings in the Grotte d'Observatoire in Monaco and paintings in the Grotte Cosquer near Marseille date from as far back as 1 million BC. Between 2500 and 2000 BC, dwellers in the Vallée des Merveilles *(see p105)* left behind carvings of beasts and human figures.

2 Foundation of Aix
In 123 BC the Phoenician Greeks, settled in Marseille since 600 BC, asked for Roman help against the invading Celtic tribes inland. After defeating the Celts, the Romans founded Aquae Sextia (Aix) in the area *(see pp14–15)*.

3 Advent of Christianity
In AD 40 St Honorat brought Christianity to Provence, founding the first monastery on Ile de Lérins. Camarguais legend, however, claims Christianity was brought here by Mary Magdalene herself *(see p60)*.

4 Franks and Saracens
With the fall of the Roman Empire in AD 476 Provence was pillaged by barbarians, eventually coming under the rule of the Franks. From the 8th century the coasts were harried by Moorish pirates who gave their name to the Massif des Maures. They were finally defeated in 974 by Guillaume le Libérateur, Count of Arles.

5 Dawn of a Dynasty
In 1297 François Grimaldi, a supporter of the papacy in the Guelph-Ghibelline feuds which beset 13th-century Italy, seized Monaco and its castle to found the dynasty which still rules there today.

6 The Avignon Papacy
Pope Clement V relocated to Avignon in 1309 to escape strife-torn Rome, the first of a succession of nine French pontiffs who were to reside in the Provençal town. In 1348 Clement VI bought the city and Avignon remained the seat of the papacy until 1377 *(see pp8–9)*.

Monastère Fortifié, built as protection against Saracen pirates

Papal Avignon

Union with France
In 1486 King René of Naples, the last of the Anjou dynasty who ruled Provence from 1246, died without issue, and most of the region became part of France. Nice and the Alpes Maritimes, however, remained part of the Kingdom of Savoy, before finally passing to France in 1860.

Plague and War
In the second half of the 16th century religious strife erupted in the Luberon between reforming Vaudois (Huguenot) factions and conservative Catholic forces. The plague of 1580 added to the region's woes.

La Marseillaise
When the French Revolution erupted in 1789, the people of Marseille were among its staunchest supporters, marching to a tune that became known as La Marseillaise, now France's national anthem.

Resistance and Liberation
After the Nazi invasion of 1940, Provence was ruled by the collaborationist Vichy government, until it was occupied by Germany in 1942. Guerrilla fighters in the *maquis* (scrubland) resisted the Occupation. On 15 August 1944, Allied troops landed, liberating Provence after two weeks of fighting.

Top 10 Figures in History

Julius Caesar
Caesar besieged Marseille after its citizens sided with his rival Pompey in 49 BC.

François Grimaldi
Grimaldi disguised his soldiers as monks in order to seize Monaco in 1297.

The Anti-pope
When the papacy returned to Rome, French cardinals elected Robert de Genève as Pope Clement VII, creating a split in the Church until 1417.

Petrarch
The Italian Renaissance poet (1304–74), who lived in Avignon, was a critic of the ostentatious French papacy.

Nostradamus
Born in St-Rémy-de-Provence, the scholar (1503–66) published his book of prophecies in 1555.

Napoleon Bonaparte
Bonaparte landed at Golfe-Juan on 1 March 1815 to regain his empire, only to be defeated at Waterloo.

Louis-Auguste Blanqui
Born in Puget-Théniers in 1805, the socialist was one of the leaders of the revolutionary Paris Commune of 1871.

Jacques Cousteau
Toulon-based naval officer Cousteau perfected the aqualung in the 1940s, pioneering the sport of scuba diving.

Antoine de St-Exupéry
The aircraft of the French author and pilot vanished in 1944 while on a reconnaissance flight over Provence.

Brigitte Bardot
Sex icon and film star Bardot became the symbol of St-Tropez in the 1960s.

Left and centre **Roman amphitheatre, Orange** Right **Arc de Triomphe, Cavaillon**

🔟 Roman Sights

1 Arles
Remnants of Provence's most important Roman settlement can still be seen around this lovely town *(see pp12–13)*.

2 Vaison-la-Romaine
Another Roman gem, discovered in 1907 *(see pp22–3)*.

3 Parc de la Colline St-Eutrope, Orange
One of the best preserved theatres from the Roman empire, built during the reign of Augustus (c.27–25 BC), is the highlight of the Parc de la Colline St-Eutrope. Nearby, a triumphal arch decorated with relief carvings commemorates Julius Caesar's victories over Gaul *(see p117)*.

4 Les Antiques de Glanum
Twin temples, a Roman forum, baths and a fortified gate can be seen at Glanum, near St-Rémy, which also reveals traces of a 4th-century Greek settlement. Another triumphal arch (10 BC) marks more Gallic victories *(see p71)*.

Triumphal arch, Glanum

5 La Trophée des Alpes
This majestic Roman monument, built from local white stone, was erected in 6 BC to mark the boundary between Italy and Gaul and to honour Augustus's Gallic conquests. Towering over the small village of La Turbie, high above Monte Carlo, with breathtaking views of the Riviera, it still has the power to impress *(see p107)*.

La Trophée des Alpes

6 Les Arènes de Fréjus
Like other large Roman arenas in Provence, the amphitheatre at Fréjus *(see p77)*, which can seat up to 10,000 people, is still used regularly for bullfights and classical music concerts. It was originally built in the 1st–2nd centuries AD. Nearby are parts of the original Roman wall. ✆ *Rue H. Vadon • Map F4 • Open Apr–Sep: 9:30am–12:30pm, 2–6pm Tue–Sun; Oct–Mar: 9:30am–noon, 2–4:30pm Tue, Thu–Sat • Closed public hols • Adm €2*

7 Arc de Triomphe, Cavaillon

This twin-arched triumphal gate, lavishly adorned with carved vines and dramatic Corinthian columns, was built during the reign of the Emperor Augustus, in the 1st century AD. There are other interesting Roman finds in the town's archaeological museum. ⊗ *Map C3*

8 Pont du Gard, Gard

The Romans considered this 49 m- (160 ft-) high three-tiered bridge to be clear testimony to their empire's greatness. The top tier was part of an aqueduct that supplied Nîmes with water for up to 500 years. Constructed from dressed stone blocks without mortar, the bridge is 275 m (900 ft) long and an enormous feat of engineering. ⊗ *Map A3*

9 Roche Taillée, Mons

This village aqueduct cut deep into solid rock is an impressive example of Roman civil engineering and an indication of how highly the Romans valued civilized comforts such as a reliable supply of running water. Those comforts unfortunately vanished with the fall of the Empire and were not regained until the 19th century. ⊗ *Map F4*

Roche Taillée aqueduct

10 Temple of Apollo, Riez

The four Corinthian columns of the 1st-century-AD temple to Apollo, standing tall and alone among fields just outside Riez on the Valensole plateau, are all that remain of the once prosperous Roman settlement of Reia Apollinaris. Eight ancient pillars, perhaps scavenged from another Roman building, are now in the early Christian church nearby, which dates from the 4th–5th century BC and is one of the oldest surviving churches in France. ⊗ *Map E3*

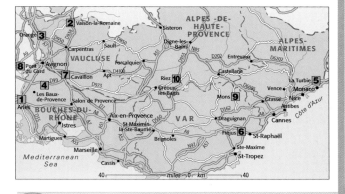

Left **Matisse drawing, Chapelle du Rosaire** Right **Abbaye de Montmajour**

Places of Worship

1 Eglise St-Trophime, Arles

An elegant interior and Romanesque carving make this the most attractive of all Provençal churches. It's also one of the oldest – a church stood here as early as AD 450. In the 11th century the church was rebuilt and dedicated to St Trophime *(see p13)*. ◈ *Pl de la République • Map B4 • Open mid-Apr–Sep: 8am–noon, 2–7pm Mon–Sat, 9am–1pm, 3–7pm Sun; Oct–mid-Apr: 8am–noon, 2–6pm daily • Closed 1 Jan, 1 May, 1 Nov, 25 Dec • Free (excl cloister)*

2 Notre-Dame-de-Beaulieu, Cucuron

A harmonious blend of Romanesque and Gothic, with a barrel-vaulted nave and rib-vaulted apse, this church dates from the 1300s. ◈ *Map H4 • Open 9am–6pm daily (to 5pm in winter) • Free*

3 Eglise de Notre-Dame, Les-Saintes-Maries-de-la-Mer

The belltower of this fortified church is a Camargue landmark. The church has lent its name to the capital of the region, and its sturdy walls offered refuge from raiders. The most colourful sight is the carved boat with statues of the Virgin and Mary Magdalene. ◈ *Map A4 • Open Apr–Nov: 3–8pm daily; Dec–Mar: 3–6pm Sat, Sun • Free*

4 Abbaye de Montmajour

The extraordinary abbey of Montmajour was built on a rocky island amid the Rhône marshes. It was an important pilgrimage site and became wealthy on its sale of pardons for sins. The cloister is decorated with mythical and Biblical scenes *(see p72)*.

5 Cathédrale, Fréjus

Constructed in the pink stone typical of Fréjus, the 13th-century cathedral has a beautiful Renaissance doorway. Its interior is dominated by superb pointed arches, and the cloister ceiling, with its scenes of the Apocalypse, is unique *(see p77)*.

6 Notre-Dame-du-Puy, Grasse

Fragonard's *Christ Washing the Disciples' Feet* is the main reason for visiting this 13th-century church. It also contains three striking religious works by Rubens, all painted in 1601: *The Crown of*

Cathédrale, Fréjus

32

Thorns, *The Crucifixion of Christ* and *The Deposition of St Helena*. ◈ *8 pl du Petit Puy* • *Map G4* • *Open 9:30–11:30am, 3–5:30pm Mon–Sat (Jul–Sep: to 6:30pm daily)* • *DA* • *Free*

7 Chapelle des Pénitents Blancs, Les-Baux-de-Provence

Frescoes in this simple chapel, painted in 1974 by local artist Yves Brayer, depict a typical Provençal nativity scene with shepherds. More of Brayer's work can be seen in the nearby museum *(see p71)*.
◈ *Map B3* • *Open Easter–Nov: 9am–6pm daily; winter hours vary* • *Free*

Notre-Dame-du-Puy, Grasse

8 Notre-Dame de l'Assomption, Puget-Théniers

Built by the Knights Templar, the 13th-century parish church of this mountain village has a lovely altarpiece, *Notre Dame de Secours* (1525) by Antoine Ronzen, and a reredos of the Passion carried out by Flemish craftsmen. ◈ *Map G3* • *Open 8am–6pm daily* • *Free*

9 Notre-Dame du Bourg, Digne-les-Bains

Lovely arched windows bring light into this striking former cathedral, probably built during the 13th century. Its west front is lavishly decorated with carved stonework. ◈ *Le Bourg* • *Map E2* • *Opening times vary; call 04 92 32 06 48 for details* • *DA* • *Free*

10 Chapelle du Rosaire de Vence

The dazzling white interior walls of this little chapel are adorned with black line drawings of the Stations of the Cross. They are unmistakably the work of Henri Matisse *(see p36)*, who designed this building in 1949. ◈ *Map G4* • *Open 2–5:30pm Mon, Wed, Sat; 10–11:30am, 2–5:30pm Tue, Thu (also Fri in Jul & Aug); Mass 10am Sun, followed by guided tour* • *Closed mid-Nov–mid-Dec* • *DA* • *Adm*

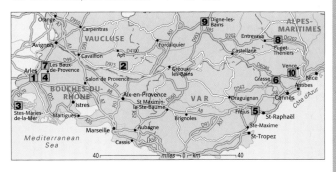

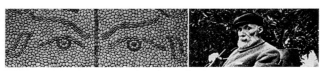

Left **Mosaic, Musée Jean Cocteau** Right **Pierre-Auguste Renoir**

Art Galleries

1 Musée de l'Annonciade, St-Tropez

This museum tops Provence's list of superb art collections. Opened in 1955, it boasts works by Pierre Bonnard, Raoul Dufy, the pointillist Paul Signac and Charles Camoin, whose work *St-Tropez, la Place des Lices et le Café des Arts* (1925) is one of the most famous images of the town *(see p18)*.
🖎 *Pl Grammont, Vieux Port • Map F5 • Open 10am–1pm, 2–6pm Wed–Mon • Closed 1 Jan, Ascension (sixth Sun after Easter), 1 May, 17 May, Nov, 25 Dec • Adm*

2 Fondation Maeght, St-Paul-de-Vence

This small museum has a world-class array of modern art, including paintings by Léger, Bonnard and Chagall, sculpture by Miró and a mosaic pool by Braque *(see p105)*.

3 Musée Matisse, Nice

The most attractive collection in Nice, the Musée Matisse, founded in 1963, nine years after the painter's death, and is in the 17th-century Villa des Arènes. There are sketches, paintings and bronze sculpture by Matisse, as well as some of his personal effects *(see p87)*.

4 Musée Picasso, Antibes

Housed in the Château Grimaldi, used as a studio by Picasso in 1946, the museum contains more than 50 of his paintings, sketches, prints and ceramics, as well as works by Léger and Miró *(see p93)*.

5 Musée National Marc Chagall, Nice

One of the jewels of Provence, this museum houses the world's largest collection of works by Marc Chagall, including 17 canvases from his Biblical Message series *(see p88)*.

6 Musée Fernand Léger, Biot

Mosaics in primary colours, carried out to Léger's own design, identify this strikingly modern museum. The Cubist painter planned to build a studio here just before his death in 1955, and the museum contains more than 400 of his works *(see p105)*.

Marteau de Porte, Aristide Maillol, Musée de l'Annonciade

7 Musée Jean Cocteau, Menton

The multi-talented Jean Cocteau, a playwright, author and film director as well as artist and designer, converted this 17th-century fort into his personal museum. It also houses

For more on painters in Provence **See pp36–7**

Musée Jean Cocteau

1,800 pieces donated by art enthusiast and Cocteau devotee Séverin Wunderman's collection.
Ⓢ 3 ave de la Madone • Map H3 • Open 10am–6pm Wed–Mon (Jul, Aug: to 10pm Fri) • Closed public hols • Adm

Musée d'Art Moderne et d'Art Contemporain, Nice

A dazzling work of contemporary architecture in its own right, with marble-faced towers and glass corridors, the contemporary art museum contains works by some of the 20th century's greatest avant-garde artists (see p87).

Musée des Beaux-Arts, Menton

Menton's museum of fine art is housed in the former summer palace of the Grimaldi princes of Monaco. Highlights include works by Utrillo, Dufy and the English painter Graham Sutherland.
Ⓢ Palais Carnolès, 3 ave de la Madone • Map H3 • Open 10am–noon, 2–6pm Wed–Mon • Closed public hols

Musée Renoir, Cagnes-sur-Mer

Auguste Renoir's house at Les Collettes, where the painter came in hope that the climate would cure his rheumatism, houses 11 of his paintings. The house is surrounded by beautiful olive groves (see p94).

Top 10 Masterpieces of Provence

1 Café du Soir
Vincent van Gogh painted more than 300 canvases in the town of Arles (see pp12–13). Café du Soir (1888) is one of the best known.

2 La Joie de Vivre
This 1946 work is one of Picasso's most important from his Antibes period.

3 La Partie de Campagne
Fernand Léger overlays bold colours on bold, comic-book outlines in this 1954 painting.

4 Nu Bleu IV
The 1952 work is among the best known of Matisse's blue paper cut-outs series.

5 St-Tropez, la Place des Lices et le Café des Arts
Charles Camoin evokes the St-Tropez of 1925.

6 L'Orage
Pointillist Paul Signac's 1895 work glowingly depicts St-Tropez harbour.

7 La Montagne Sainte-Victoire au Grand Pin
This 1887 painting is one of Cézanne's most renowned images of the Provence mountain (see p15).

8 The Burning Bush
Nicolas Froment's 1476 triptych in the Cathédrale de St-Saveur (see p14) was commissioned by Provence's last king, René.

9 Jetée Promenade à Nice
Portraying an evening stroll on the esplanade, the 1928 work is Dufy at his colourful best.

10 Venus Victrix
One of Renoir's finest bronzes (1914) stands amid the olive groves at Les Collettes.

Left **Jetée d'Honfleur, Raoul Dufy** Right **Self Portrait, Pablo Picasso**

Painters in Provence

1 Paul Cézanne

Born in Aix, where he lived most of his life, Cézanne (1839–1906) painted hundreds of oil and watercolour scenes of his home town and the nearby Mont Sainte-Victoire (see pp14–15) in his own Post-Impressionist style. Better than any other painter, he captures the soul of Provence.

2 Vincent van Gogh

The Dutch master (1854–90) created hundreds of his vivid, powerful landscapes and self-portraits during his few years in Arles and St-Rémy. The sunshine of Provence changed the way Van Gogh saw light and colour.

3 Pablo Picasso

The driving force behind the Cubist movement, Picasso (1881–1973) was influenced by the sights and colours of Provence, where he lived in exile from his native Spain for much of his life. He learned to make ceramics from the potters of Vallauris and helped revive the craft (see p100).

4 Henri Matisse

Matisse (1869–1954) lived in Nice from 1917 until his death. His earlier works were inspired by the vivid light and colours of the Riviera. During World War II he retreated to Vence, where he designed the unique Chapelle du Rosaire, including its wonderful vestments and furnishings (see p33).

5 Paul Signac

The masterful exponent of pointillist style, Signac (1863–1935) came to St-Tropez in 1892. He found, in the glittering reflection of sun on sea, the perfect subject for pointillism's technique of using a myriad of tiny rainbow dots to depict swathes or blocks of colour, giving an almost psychedelic effect.

6 Marc Chagall

The Russian-born painter (1887–1985) moved to St-Paul-de-Vence in 1949. His light-filled work was often inspired by Biblical themes, and canvases from his Biblical Message series of paintings are in the Musée National Message Biblique Marc Chagall in Nice (see p88).

La Montagne Sainte-Victoire, Paul Cézanne

For the Top 10 art galleries in Provence See pp34–5

Lilac Bush, Vincent van Gogh

Fernand Léger

Léger (1881–1955) is known for his strong Cubist paintings and his love of bold lines and pure primary colours. First a figurative painter, he worked in the Cubist style before returning to painting that seems to echo poster or graphic art.

Yves Klein

Born in Iceland, Klein (1928–62) became one of the leading lights of the Nice School of new realists, who aimed to create art from everyday materials. His *Anthropométries*, in Nice's Musée d'Art Moderne et d'Art Contemporain *(see p87)*, was created by three paint-covered nude women rolling over a huge white canvas.

Raoul Dufy

Dufy (1877–1955) embodies the values of the Fauvist school, with its revolutionary use of bright, intense colour. He found Nice the perfect background for his vivid work.

Paul Guigou

This realist painter (1834–71) painted sunny landscapes of his native Vaucluse, capturing the pure light of Provence's rugged hillsides. Among his best known works is *Deux Lavandières devant la Sainte-Victoire*, on display in the Musée Grobet-Labadié in Marseille *(see p66)*.

Top 10 Writers in Provence

Frédéric Mistral

This Nobel Prize-winner (1830–1914) wrote epic poems based on local lore.

Alexandre Dumas

Dumas (1802–70) used the Château d'If *(see p67)* as the grim backdrop to *The Count of Monte Cristo* (1845).

Victor Hugo

Hugo (1802–85) set the early chapters of his epic novel *Les Misérables* (1862) in Digne-les-Bains.

Albert Camus

This French author and existentialist (1913–60) wrote his autobiography at Lourmarin.

Alphonse Daudet

Daudet (1849–97) is best remembered for *Tartarin de Tarascon*, the tale of a Provençal bumpkin *(see p60)*.

Graham Greene

The English novelist (1914–91) retired to Nice, where he wrote *J'Accuse – the Dark Side of Nice* (1982).

F. Scott Fitzgerald

The US writer (1896–1940) stayed at Juan-les-Pins in 1926 to write his novel *Tender is the Night*.

Ernest Hemingway

Another US visitor to Provence, Hemingway (1898–1961) set *The Garden of Eden* in La Napoule.

Marcel Pagnol

The French author and film director (1895–1974) wrote *L'Eau des Collines* (1963), later filmed as *Jean de Florette* and *Manon des Sources*.

Colette

Colette (1873–1954) wrote charmingly of St-Tropez in *La Naissance du Jour* (1928).

Left **Bormes-les-Mimosas** Centre **Fontaine-de-Vaucluse** Right **St-Paul-de-Vence**

🔟 Provence Villages

1 Moustiers-Ste-Marie
At the entrance to the Verdon gorges (see pp10–11), Moustiers hangs like a pendant from the rock-face soaring above (see p112). The glorious tangle of vaulted streets, tiny squares and tiled roofs is divided by rushing streams. Up above, tucked against the rocks, is the Notre-Dame-de-Beauvoir chapel (see p11). The village is also celebrated for its pottery.

Chapel, Les-Baux-de-Provence

2 Les-Baux-de-Provence
Emerging dramatically from its crag on the edge of the Alpilles hills, Les-Baux was home to one of the finest courts in medieval Provence. Abandoned for centuries, the ruined castle and labyrinthine streets now throb with summer tourists. But the site remains majestic, the atmosphere lively and the views over mountains and plains quite breathtaking (see p71).

3 St-Paul-de-Vence
St-Paul was a farming community living quietly within its medieval surroundings and 16th-century walls until the 1920s. Then it was discovered by the Côte d'Azur artistic community (Picasso, Matisse, Léger) and has been fashionable ever since, with good reason. Both artists and tourists find the tiny streets, ramparts and church remains utterly charming (see p108).

4 Fontaine-de-Vaucluse
The "fontaine" is actually Europe's most powerful natural spring – it pumps out 2.5 million cubic m (55 million gallons) of water a day, giving birth to the River Sorgue. It's a spectacular setting for a lovely village, made even more romantic by its association with the Italian love poet, Petrarch, who lived here in the 14th century (see p118).

5 Bormes-les-Mimosas
This delightful village seems to tumble down the hillside, its jumble of steep alleys, hidden corners and stone houses overcome with flowers – the village name tells no lies. Climb to the top and the views to the sea from the ruined medieval castle are splendid (see p79).

6 Roussillon
Roussillon is perched beautifully above a quite extraordinary landscape. The mining of ochre and subsequent erosion have

sculpted the red-and-gold earth into cliffs, canyons and weird shapes. Villagers have applied the local product to their houses, to enchanting effect *(see p123)*.

7 Séguret
Encircling its hillside like a belt, Séguret stares out from the edges of the Dentelles de Montmirail mountains across the nearby wine plain. It's an almost impossibly pretty spot of tiny, pedestrianized streets, medieval edifices and contemporary artists and artisans *(see p123)*.

8 Cassis
Cassis is overseen by France's highest coastal cliffs, whose scale reinforces the intimacy of the narrow little harbour and old town centre down below. Tourists crowd the beaches – the best bathing is in the creeks to the west – but Cassis remains a fishing port, and well retains its authenticity *(see p72)*.

9 Sisteron
At the northern gateway to Provence, Sisteron's minuscule vaulted streets and unexpected staircases climb the vast sentinel

Sisteron

rock overlooking the River Durance. It's a harsh setting for a village with a strong past. Up top, the 14th-century citadel was all but impregnable and now affords unbeatable views over the rugged landscape *(see p111)*.

10 Roquebrune-Cap-Martin
A winning partnership of the sort only found on the Côte d'Azur. Beneath Roquebrune are the grandiose *belle époque* villas of the super-rich on the Cap-Martin peninsula. Up above are the winding streets, vaulted passages and 10th-century chateau of the original village *(see p95)*.

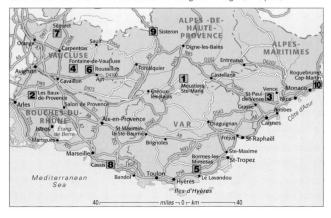

Left **Camargue cowboy** Right **Les Alpilles**

Areas of Natural Beauty

1 The Camargue

A landscape of lagoons, marshes, wild bulls and Europe's only cowboys *(see pp20–21).*

2 Parc National du Mercantour

Mercantour National Park, sprawling over 700 sq km (270 sq miles), is one of Europe's largest and its rocky slopes are home to rare species including chamois, ibex, moufflon and marmot. Golden eagles and the rare lammergeier vulture soar above the peaks *(see p105).* ◈ *Map G2*

Mont Ventoux

3 Parc Naturel Régional du Luberon

The Luberon region contains a wide range of habitats. The northern mountains are wild and exposed, while the central massif shelters the southern slopes, creating a gentler environment. Moorland, cedar forest, chalk hills and deep river gorges shelter wild boar, eagles, owls and beavers *(see p117).*

4 Parc National de Port-Cros

Port-Cros is the smallest of the Îles d'Hyères, and the national park protects the delightful island and 18 sq km (7 sq miles) of sea around it from the development that has overtaken so much of the coast. On land, it shelters beautiful butterflies and rare sea birds, and there is excellent scuba diving and snorkelling *(see p83).* ◈ *Map E6*

5 Mont Ventoux

The lonely peak of Mont Ventoux, at 1,910 m (6,260 ft), seems to guard the gateway to the region. Bare of trees, its higher slopes are known as the *désert de pierre* (stone desert) and are snow-covered from December to April. It has featured in the Tour de France, and even the strongest cyclists dread the treacherous ascent *(see p119).*

6 Les Alpilles

The chalky hills of the "Little Alps" rise no higher than 500 m (1,640 ft) but display an arid beauty. This miniature sierra stretches for 24 km (15 miles) between the rivers Rhône and Durance, and the GR6 hiking trail which crosses it is one of the finest walks in Provence *(see p129).* ◈ *Map B4*

7 Gorges du Cians and Gorges du Dalius

High in the mountains of Haute-Provence and the Alpes-Maritimes, the parallel canyons

For walks in Provence **See p57**

of the Gorges du Cians and the Gorges du Dalius are awesome ravines, carved by icy fast-flowing streams running down from wine-red cliffs. The main landmark is the Gardienne des Gorges, a huge boulder shaped like a woman's head, standing at the north end of the Gorges du Dalius *(see p106)*.

Farmers, Massif des Maures

Gorges du Loup
The clifftop village of Gourdon, set in rugged limestone country, stands above the dramatic Gorges du Loup, the most accessible of the gorges and canyons that slash through this craggy landscape. The Loup stream plunges over high cascades and has carved deep potholes such as the Saut du Loup ("Wolf's Leap") *(see p106)*.

Massif des Maures
Thickly wooded with forests of cork and holm oak, pine, myrtle and sweet chestnut, the dramatic Massif des Maures is wild, hilly and sparsely inhabited,

even though it is only a stone's throw from the busy coastal hotspots. It is home to France's only surviving wild tortoises, and makes a welcome change from crowded beaches *(see p79)*.

Réserve Géologique de Haute-Provence
If dinosaurs and fossils are your thing, this park in the limestone country around Digne is the place to head for. It's the largest of its kind in Europe, covering 1,900 sq km (730 sq miles) of rock, rich in fossils from ancient seas and tropical forests dating back 300 million years. ◈ *Map F2*

Left **Summer on the Riviera** Right **Hillside view over the Riviera**

Beaches in Provence

1 Notre Dame Beach, Ile de Porquerolles

No cars are allowed on the island, so it's a walk or cycle-ride along the rocky, 3-km (2-mile) track from the port to the loveliest beach in France *(see p83)*. Pine-fringed, it boasts white sand, calm waters, no commerce and few people. Your private slice of paradise. ◈ *Map E6*

Pampelonne Beach, St-Tropez

2 Pampelonne Beach, St-Tropez

Everyone has his or her "place" on St-Trop's largest beach. Famous beach clubs cater to the super-rich and glamorous, to nudists, to gays, as well as to everyday families. The 5-km (3-mile) sandy stretch across the headland from the town also has extensive public areas. There's space in which to escape the crowds and appreciate natural beauty *(see p19)*. ◈ *Map F5*

3 Calanque d'En-Vau, Cassis

"*Calanques*" are inlets formed where the chalk cliffs plunge to the sea, many are found between Cassis and Marseille. En-Vau is the prettiest and one of the more accessible – a mere 90-minute walk from the nearest Cassis car park. At the foot of the white, pine-clad rocks, the setting of sand and luminous sea is intimate, wild and quite unforgettable *(see p66)*.

4 Elephant Beach, Le Lavandou

Le Lavandou has a total of 12 beaches, covering the full seaside spectrum, from the great sandy stretch of the Grande Plage to the nudist creek of Rossignol. Most appealing of all, however, is l'Eléphant. The approach is only by sea or by scrambling over rocks, a feature which usually ensures relative tranquillity. ◈ *Map F5*

Le Lavandou beach

For beach activities in Provence **See p83 & p98**

5 Calanque de Figuerolles, La Ciotat

Steps on the eastern edge of town lead down to this extra-ordinary creek. On either side are cliffs, while further back are terraces of fig-trees and pines. Out front, the blue sea laps around weird rock formations and onto the pebble shore. A world unto itself. ✎ Map D5

6 La Garoupe Beach, Cap-d'Antibes

Between them, Antibes and Juan-les-Pins have 25 km (16 miles) of coast and 48 beaches, slotted into rocky creeks or opening out into sandy expanses. The prettiest is La Garoupe, on an inlet of the peninsula. It's highly fashionable and, in summer, very crowded – but with good reason. ✎ Map G4

7 Agay Beach, St-Raphaël

As the red rocks of the Esterel hills tumble into the clear blue sea, they give the coast around St-Raphaël an untamed allure. The small creeks are enticing; equally alluring, but bigger, sandier and more acces-sible, is the Bay of Agay – perfect for families (see p98).

8 St-Honorat Beaches, Iles de Lérins

A short ferry ride leads from the crowds of Cannes to this island owned by Cistercian monks. The presence of the monastery seems to discourage more brazen holidaymakers so the pretty rock outcrops and tiny beaches remain calm and, unusually for Provence, under-populated. ✎ Map G4

9 St-Aygulf Beach

Long, wide, sandy and safe, the main beach at St-Aygulf, near Fréjus (see p77), has the additional advantage of being in a Nature Preservation Area. This protects the Etangs de Villepey – great, wild, freshwater lagoons on the other side of the road, where 217 different bird species have been noted. A beautiful setting. ✎ Map G5

Camargue beach

10 Piémançon Beach, The Camargue

This is the beach beyond civilization. You must thread around salt-flats and lagoons before arriving at the flat, exposed sands. Life is a little rugged, but ideal for wilder beach elements. ✎ Map B5

Left **Port-Cros, Iles d'Hyères** Right **Ste-Marguérite, Iles de Lérins**

🔟 Offshore Islands

Porquerolles, Iles d'Hyères
The largest of the French Riviera islands is the car-free idyll of Porquerolles. Hire a bike or explore on foot to appreciate this paradise of vineyards, olive groves, scented forests and glorious beaches. ⚲ *Map E6 • Ferry from La Tour-Fondue, near Giens*

Port Cros, Iles d'Hyères
A national park, the smallest and most mountainous of the Hyères isles is dense with pine woods and oaks. Paths lead up to clifftops with dramatic views. La Palud is the best beach.
⚲ *Map F6 • Ferry from Hyères*

Le Levant, Iles d'Hyères
Although 90 per cent of this island is a French Navy missile base, the other 10 per cent is a naturist colony. Clothes must be worn in the village but not beyond. ⚲ *Map F6 • Ferry from Hyères*

Iles de Frioul
The islands of Ratonneau and Pomègues guard Marseille harbour *(see p65)*. Beyond Port Frioul, white rocks ruggedly conceal little beaches. The diving here is renowned. ⚲ *Map C5 • Ferry from Vieux Port, Marseille*

Ile d'If
This prison island is most famous as the place from which the fictional Count of Monte Cristo escaped *(see p37)*. You may even visit the "Count's dungeon". ⚲ *Map C5 • Ferry from Vieux Port, Marseille*

Ste-Marguérite, Iles de Lérins
Ste-Marguérite offers woods of pine and eucalyptus and little stony beaches. In 1687 the Man In The Iron Mask was imprisoned in the island's fort *(see p60)*.
⚲ *Map G4 • Ferry from Cannes harbour*

Iles d'Hyères coastline

All the islands are closed to cars

Fort, Ste-Marguerite

St-Honorat, Iles de Lérins

A smaller version of Ste-Marguerite, St-Honorat has been run by monks almost continually since the 5th century. The 11th-century fortified monastery is a must-see. ❧ *Map G4 • 04 92 99 54 00 • Ferry from Cannes harbour • Fortified monastery: Open Jul–19 Sep: 10am–noon, 2:30–5pm daily; 20 Sep–Jun: 7am–6pm daily • www.abbayedelerins.com*

Iles des Embiez

The larger of two islands developed for tourism by drinks magnate Paul Ricard, Embiez is a delight. Development has been merged into the landscape, leaving most of the island's creeks, woods and salt marshes untouched. ❧ *Map D6 • Ferry from Le Brusc, near Six-Fours-les-Plages • www.les-embiez.com*

Bendor

Embiez's baby brother has a tiny harbour and beaches – you can do the tour in 20 minutes. But the tourist development is as sensitive as on Embiez, marrying the landscape extremely naturally. ❧ *Map D5 • Ferry from Bandol*

Ile Verte

"Verte" refers to the island's greenery, notably the trees topping the steep cliffs. Billed as "one of the last virgin islands of the Mediterranean coast", the islet has tiny creeks and beaches. ❧ *Map D5 • Ferry from La Ciotat old port*

Top 10 Island Activities

1 Cycling

On Porquerolles and Embiez, cycle the forest paths to creeks and beaches.

2 Scuba-diving, Port Cros

A guided underwater "trail" offers marine-life close-ups. ❧ *National Park Office • 04 94 01 40 70 • www.port crosparcnational.fr*

3 Fort Ste-Agathe, Porquerolles

Exhibitions on the region's nature. ❧ *Open mid-May–Sep: 10am–12:30pm, 1:30–5pm • 04 94 58 07 24 • Adm • www.porquerolles.com*

4 Diving, Embiez

Courses held in water rich with marine life. ❧ *Centre de Plongée • 04 94 34 12 78*

5 Lighthouse Walk, Porquerolles

A 90-minute round trip to one of the finest lighthouses.

6 Fort de l'Estissac, Port Cros

Exhibits on local history. ❧ *Open Apr–Sep: 10:30am–5pm*

7 Aquascope, Embiez

Glass "bubble" over water allows close encounters of a marine kind. ❧ *Open Jul–Oct • 04 94 34 17 85 • Adm*

8 Sailing, Bendor

Sailing classes all year round. ❧ *Club Nautique de Bendor • 04 94 29 52 91*

9 Vallon de la Solitude Walk, Port Cros

A 2-hour walk through shady forest to the Fort de la Vigie.

10 Universal Wine and Spirits Exhibition, Bendor

Display of 8,000 bottles from 51 countries. ❧ *Open Jul–Aug: 1–6pm Thu–Tue • 04 94 29 44 34 • www.euvs.org • Free*

Left & Centre **Jardins d'Albertas, Bouc-Bel-Air** Right **Jardins du Château, Ansouis**

Gardens of Provence

1 Domaine du Rayol, le Rayol-Canadel

On one of the most magnificent sites on the coast, Rayol offers an overview of Mediterranean-style plant life. Gathered around a pergola and long stairway, a fine mosaic of eight gardens recreates landscapes of areas of the world with Mediterranean climates. ◎ *Ave des Belges • Map F5 • Open from 9:30am daily, call ahead for closing: 04 98 04 44 00 • DA • Adm*

2 Jardin de la Villa Ephrussi de Rothschild, St-Jean-Cap-Ferrat

Baroness Rothschild's mansion is legendary *(see p93)*, and its gardens of similar sumptuousness. Seven themed areas (Spanish, Florentine, Japanese and more) are rich with plants, sculptures and fountains *(see pp 93 & 99)*.

3 Jardins d'Albertas, Bouc-Bel-Air

Laid out in the 1750s, these terraced gardens remain a majestic mix of French and Italian influences – ordered in the geometrical style of France, but with the fountains and statuary favoured by Italy. ◎ *RN 8 • Map D4 • 04 42 22 94 71 • Open May, Sep, Oct: 2–6pm weekends and pub hols; Jun–Aug: 3–7pm daily • Adm • www.jardinsalbertas.com*

4 Chartreuse de Bonpas, Caumont-sur-Durance

The ruins of a fortified monastery provide a superb setting for two terraces. The first is a formal layout of yew and box-trees, shaded by Aleppo pines. The second features a lovely fountain and cascade. ◎ *Map B3 • Open 10am–12:30pm, 2–6:30pm Mon–Fri, 10am–6:30pm Sat, Sun • Closed Jan–Mar: Mon, Tue • Adm*

5 Serre de la Madone, Menton

Anglo-American Lawrence Johnston was a leader among expats who left their mark on Riviera gardens in the early 20th century. His hillside spread is so well landscaped, it barely seems structured at all. Terraces harbour enclosed spaces dedicated to themes or particular exotic plants, and there are fountains, water-gardens and a collection of statues.

Jardins du Château, Ansouis

◈ *74 rte de Gorbio • Map H3 • 04 93 57 73 90 • Open 10am–6pm Tue–Sun (to 5pm Dec–Mar); guided tours 3pm daily • Closed 1 Jan, Nov, 25 Dec • Adm • www.serredelamadone.com*

6 Jardins du Château, Ansouis

The medieval chateau, which was remodelled during the Renaissance, is flanked by terraces, each with sculpted box-trees, overseen by firs and pines. ◈ *Rue Cartel • Map C3 • 06 84 62 64 34 • Open Apr–Nov: guided tours only, 2:20pm, 3:30pm, 4:30pm Tue–Sun • Adm*

7 Jardin Botanique Exotique du Val Rahmeh, Menton

More than 700 tropical plants crowd these terraces, established in 1905 by Lord Radcliff, a former governor of Malta. Val Rahmeh specializes in spices, wildflowers, medicinal plants and rare varieties of tomato and potato. ◈ *Ave St Jacques • Map H3 • Open 10am–12:30pm, 2–5pm Wed–Mon (Apr–Sep: 10am–12:30pm, 3:30–6:30pm) • Closed 1 May • Adm*

8 Jardin Exotique, Monaco

A collection of cactuses, succulents and other semi-desert plants – 6,000 varieties in all. Criss-crossed by a winding path, it is said to be the world's largest such rockery *(see p99)*.

Jardin Exotique, Monaco

9 Parc Olbius Riquier, Hyères

This 17-acre (7-ha) park has a varied collection of trees: canary pines, ginkgo biloba, agave and a great selection of palms. There's a little zoo and, in the glasshouse, tropical plants and exotic birds. ◈ *Ave Ambroise Thomas • Map E6 • 04 94 00 78 65 • Open from 7:30am daily (closing times vary) • DA • Free*

10 Jardin Botanique des Cordeliers, Digne-les-Bains

The garden has a classical design, planted in squares for the growing of aromatic plants for essences and medicines. More than 650 species recall the importance of plants in Provençal life. ◈ *Ave Paul Martin • Map E2 • Open mid-Mar–mid-Nov: 9am–noon, 2–6pm Mon–Fri (to 7pm Jul–Aug) • Guided tours in English by appt: 04 92 31 59 59 • DA • Free*

For Top 10 Riviera gardens **See p99**

Left **Café posing** Right **La Colombe d'Or, St-Paul-de-Vence**

⚙10 Places to See and Be Seen

1 Carlton InterContinental, Cannes

The spacious terrace in front of the Carlton InterContinental, one of Cannes' exorbitantly luxurious seafront hotels, overlooks the Croisette and is the top place to see and be seen in town, with a magnificent view of the bay. For effect, drink Bollinger *(see p102)*.

2 Zélo, Beaulieu Port

Don your best bikini and sashay down to one of the Riviera's hippest beaches, which attracts a star-studded crowd. Sunbeds start at €25 for half a day; there's a restaurant, Wi-Fi and late-night partying. ⊗ *Port de Plaisance, Promenade Pasteur • Map H4 • 04 93 91 97 34 or 04 93 01 11 00 • DA*

3 Le Petit Majestic, Cannes

This late night hangout is popular with the stay-up-late crowd, who party until the early hours all summer long. During the film festival you'll also find the cream of the world's movie business here *(see p58)*. ⊗ *6 rue Tony Allard • Map G4 • 04 93 39 94 92*

4 Majestic Hotel, Cannes

One of the flashiest café-terraces attracts some of the world's brightest stars – Roman Polanski, Jude Law and Gabriel Byrne have been sighted – during the film festival and a high-spending, fashionable clientele year-round. Anything stronger than coffee costs a fortune *(see p102)*.

5 Hotel du Cap Eden Roc, Antibes

Book years ahead to mingle with the rich and famous at this luxurious hotel – the flagship of Riviera hedonism. The list of celebrity guests stretches back decades and includes such current stars as Gwyneth Paltrow and Leonardo Di Caprio *(see p140)*.

La Palme d'Or, Cannes

For more luxury hotels **See pp140–41**

6 La Colombe d'Or, St-Paul-de-Vence

This celebrity hideaway hotel and restaurant attracts fashionable artists and celebrities and has a fine private collection of paintings by 20th-century artists including Miró, Matisse and Picasso. By Riviera standards, La Colombe d'Or is also surprisingly affordable – an overnight stay here need cost no more than an evening drink in one of the flashier clubs in Cannes or Monaco. *Pl de Gaulle • Map G4 • 04 93 32 80 02 • €€€€€*

Les Caves du Roy, St-Tropez

7 Les Caves du Roy, St-Tropez

To mingle with the rich and famous, book a room at St-Trop's most fashionable hotel and swan into Les Caves du Roy, the hotel's nightclub. Les Caves in season is the haunt of supermodels, film stars and racing drivers. Wear your most fabulous outfit *(see p84).*

8 Club 55, Ramatuelle, St-Tropez

Ever since Le Cinquante Cinq first opened in 1955, its guest list has been like reading an A to Z of the rich and famous. Book ahead if you want a table in the restaurant, dress to impress and bring your platinum credit card. Open summer only. *Plage de Pampelonne, blvd Patch • Map F5 • 04 94 55 55 55 • DA • €€€€€*

9 La Palme d'Or, Cannes

The restaurant at the Hotel Martinez is where stars dine, as the signed photos in the foyer attest. The menu is suitably

opulent, with lobster and foie gras. Dress to kill and prepare to reach your credit card limit *(see p51).*

10 L'Oasis, La Napoule

In a Neo-Gothic villa, overlooking La Napoule port, culinary magic is performed by the three Raimbault brothers: Stéphane, Antoine and François who take desserts to a higher dimension. The rooftop bistro offers menus at more affordable prices. *Rue Jean-Honoré-Carle • Map G4 • 04 93 49 95 52 • Closed mid-Nov–mid-Jan, Mon, Sun (Oct–Apr) • €€€€€ (bistro €€–€€€)*

Left **La Palme d'Or, Cannes** Right **Louis XV, Monte Carlo**

🔟 Gourmet Restaurants

1 Louis XV, Monte Carlo
The world's most glamorous diners expect splendour, and get it amid wood-panelling, gilt mirrors and glistening chandeliers. On the plates, too, as France's leading chefs work Provençale cuisine into an art form. If you have to think about the cost, you're in the wrong place. ◈ *Hôtel de Paris, pl du Casino • Map H4 • 003 77 98 06 88 64 • Closed Tue, Wed (except mid-Jun–Sep), late Feb–mid-Mar, Dec • DA • €€€€€*

2 Le Petit Nice Passédat, Marseille
Perched on a cliff overlooking the Med, this luxury hotel houses Marseille's first three-star Michelin restaurant. Try beignets of sea anemones or the line-caught sea bass, followed by a delicious dark chocolate and raspberry delight. ◈ *Anse de Maldormé, Corniche J-F Kennedy • Map J6 • 04 91 59 25 92 • Closed Sun–Mon, 1–20 Jan, Feb school hols & Nov • DA • €€€€€*

3 Le Chantecler, Nice
Within the palatial Negresco hotel *(see p140)*, Le Chantecler boasts Regency decor and wood panelling. The taste is exquisite, as is chef Jean-Denis Rieubland's imaginative food, such as brill glazed with lobster butter and foie gras with pomegranate jelly *(see p91)*.

4 La Bastide de Capelongue, Bonnieux
Young chef Edouard Loubet already has a huge reputation for Provençale cooking of great finesse. The surroundings are equally fine *(see p125)*.

5 Atelier Rabanel, Arles
Unusual creations from Jean-Luc Rabanel, the first organic chef to receive a Michelin star. The menu changes regularly, depending on what vegetables have been picked from the restaurant's garden, and the chef's imagination. ◈ *7 rue des Carmes • Map B4 • 04 90 91 07 69 • Closed Mon–Tue, last week in Feb • DA • €€€€€*

6 Clos de la Violette, Aix
Noted for its skilful use of flavours. Red mullet with polenta and a bouillabaisse reduction is one of the simpler dishes eaten in the dining room or, in summer, in the shaded garden *(see p75)*.

Le Petit Nice Passédat, Marseille

Bastide St Antoine, Grasse

La Mirande, Avignon

La Mirande was a cardinal's mansion during the popes' time in Avignon, then a sober town house. The restaurant offers inventive cooking of the highest class. ◈ *4 pl de la Mirande • Map B3 • 04 90 14 20 20 • Closed Tue, Wed, Jan • DA • €€€€€*

La Palme d'Or, Cannes

The restaurant of the Hotel Martinez is where the film-making classes go for the best food in town, including Provençale specialities like wild sea bass perfumed with herbs. ◈ *73 blvd de la Croisette • Map G4 • 04 92 98 74 14 • Closed Sun–Tue • DA • €€€€€*

Bastide St Antoine, Grasse

The restored 18th-century country house is superbly sited amid lavender and olive trees above Grasse. Equally splendid is the cooking of chef Jacques Chibois *(see p109)*.

L'Oustau de Baumanière, Les-Baux-de-Provence

This converted farmstead dates from the 14th century; the two-Michelin-starred food mixes the rusticity of fresh, seasonal local produce with top-class cuisine. ◈ *CD 27 • Map B4 • 04 90 54 33 07 • Closed Dec–Feb • €€€€€*

Provence's Top 10

Top 10 Regional Specialities

1 Bouillabaisse Marseille fish dish of up to six species, such as monkfish and John Dory. Spicy stock is served first as soup.

2 Salade Niçoise Purists use only raw vegetables, hard-boiled eggs, anchovies and olive oil. Others add tuna.

3 Olives Signature Provençal product. Introduced by the Greeks in the 4th century BC, olive oil is central to regional dishes.

4 Aïoli Garlic mayonnaise made with olive oil. Accompanies raw vegetables, cold cod and hard-boiled eggs.

5 Pistou Thick soup of white, red and kidney beans, pasta and other vegetables, flavoured with basil, garlic and olive oil.

6 Pieds et paquets Lamb's feet *(pieds)* and stuffed sheep's stomach *(paquets)* in white wine.

7 Ratatouille Stew of red peppers, courgettes (zucchini), aubergines (eggplant), tomatoes and onions, sautéed in olive oil.

8 Truffles Hunting of the highly flavoured underground fungus runs mid-November to mid-March. Carpentras is the centre *(see p118)*.

9 Daube Beef (or wild boar) marinated and simmered in red wine, herbs and garlic.

10 Tapenade Purée of olives, capers and anchovies, spread on toast. *Anchoïade* is similar, but without capers.

Left **Henri de Saint-Victor, owner of Château de Pibarnon** Right **Grenache vines, Provence**

Vineyards and Distilleries

Château Ste-Roseline
The chateau's Côtes-de-Provence wines have improved greatly in recent times. Its Cuvée Prieuré can age for 15 years or more, making it more than worthy of its historic surroundings. The superb chateau and grounds host summer concerts. ✆ *Sauteraine, Les-Arcs-sur-Argens • Map F4 • 04 94 99 50 30*

Château de Berne
British-owned Berne is the region's best wine visitors' centre. The site is picturesque, the welcome friendly, and there's a full calendar of cultural events. There's also a first-class hotel-restaurant on-site, L'Auberge. The best wine is the Cuvée Spéciale. ✆ *Route de Salerne, Lorgues • Map F4 • 04 94 60 43 52*

Château Romanin
If the stunning underground winery resembles a cathedral, it's not coincidental. The site has had spiritual associations since the Greeks worshipped here in the 4th century BC. The owners aim to harmonize with this past, even programming cultivation by the phases of the moon. The wines, though, are anything but eccentric. ✆ *Mas Romanin, St-Rémy-de-Provence • Map B3 • 04 90 92 45 87*

Domaine Rabiéga
In a wooded residential suburb, this Swedish-run domain has an innovative attitude to wine quality. The Cuvée Clos d'Ière is among the most expressive of Provençal wines. The welcome at the cellar is both easy and relaxed. There are also two hotels and a restaurant. ✆ *Clos d'Ière, 516 Chemin Cros d'Aimar, Draguignan • Map F4 • 04 94 68 44 22*

Distilleries & Domaines de Provence
Home of Henri Bardouin, the connoisseur's *pastis*. Like all *pastis*, Bardouin is based on star anise, but here they add 50 other herbs and spices, many of them local. The result is an apéritif more richly flavoured than other brands. ✆ *9 ave St Promasse, Forcalquier • Map D3 • www.distilleries-provence.com*

Château de Pibarnon

Domaine de la Citadelle

6 Former film producer and politician Yves Rousset-Rouard sunk a fortune into this stylish set-up. The Côtes-de-Luberon wines are treated with respect, and the on-site Corkscrew Museum is unique. Ⓢ *Route de Cavaillon, Ménerbes • Map C3 • 04 90 72 41 58*

Domaine de Beaurenard

7 The Coulon family have been in Provence's most famous wine village since 1695 – time enough to perfect their skills. The Boisrenard red is the proof. They also run the Musée du Vigneron, the region's best wine museum. Ⓢ *10 ave Pierre de Luxembourg, Châteauneuf-du-Pape • Map B3 • 04 90 83 71 79*

Domaine St André de Figuière

8 In a superb location, set back from the sea and next to a bird sanctuary, Alain Combard and his family make wines of great finesse. The visitors' entrance to the cellar is round the back of a steel tank. Ⓢ *BP47, Quartier St Honoré, La Londe-les-Maures • Map E5 • 04 94 00 44 70*

Château de l'Aumérade

9 The quintessential Provence wine domain: the wines, especially the rosés, show true Provençal character. The visit includes a museum dedicated to the region's traditional *santon* figurines *(see p134)*. Ⓢ *Pierrefeu-du-Var • Map E5 • 04 94 28 20 31*

Château de Pibarnon

10 Perched directly above the sea, this may be the most attractively sited wine chateau in Provence. Owner Henri de Saint-Victor has wrestled the unyielding land to produce red wines in the forefront of the Bandol appellation. Ⓢ *Comte de St Victor, La Cadière-d'Azur • Map D5 • 04 94 90 12 73*

Top 10 Regional Wines

1 **Châteauneuf-du-Pape**
At their best, the reds are dark and powerful, the (rarer) whites intensely fruity.

2 **Bandol**
The home of the mourvèdre grape produces fine and vigorous reds.

3 **Beaumes de Venise**
France's richest fortified dessert wine, made from the muscat grape.

4 **Côtes-de-Provence**
Famed for rosés, but now also producing classy reds and heady whites.

5 **Gigondas**
Sometimes known as "son of Châteauneuf-du-Pape" but the full-bodied wines definitely stand out on their own.

6 **Côteaux d'Aix-en-Provence**
Fast improving red and rosé wines.

7 **Cassis**
Fresh, dry whites – particularly good served with Provençale fish dishes.

8 **Côtes du Ventoux**
The reds, especially, can be very rewarding – although rosés are great for summer picnics.

9 **Côtes du Luberon**
Another hugely improved group of wines, not least due to investment from fashionable outsiders.

10 **Côtes-du-Rhône Villages**
In theory, one step up from ordinary Côtes-du-Rhône, but they can be several steps up in practice – especially if the name of the village (such as Cairanne) is mentioned on the label.

Left **Perfume distillation, Grasse** Right **Valensole Plateau**

Fragrant Provençal Sights

1 Sault-en-Provence

When the lavender flowers in July and August, the valley below the little town presents one of the loveliest landscapes in France. It's a tapestry of blue and purple, together with yellow broom, golden cereals and white rock. The town has an excellent Lavender Garden. ✆ *Distillerie Aroma Plantes, Rte de Mont Ventoux • Map C3 • Open 10am–noon, 2–6pm daily (Jun & Sep: to 7pm; Jul & Aug: 10am–7pm) • Closed 1 Jan, 15 Aug, 25 Dec*

2 Prieuré de Salagon, Mane

This Romanesque priory, dating from the 1100s, is at the centre of exceptional gardens showing the history of Provence's relationship with its plant life. They range from the Middle Ages to today and include a Garden of Aromatic Scents. An exhibition tells the story of aromatic plants. ✆ *Le Plan • Map D3 • Open Feb–Apr, Oct–mid-Dec: 10am–6pm Wed–Mon; May, Sep: 10am–7pm daily; Jun–Aug: 10am–8pm daily • Closed mid-Dec–Jan • DA • Adm*

Lavender bouquets

3 Jardin Botanique des Cordeliers, Digne-les-Bains

A history-based herb garden in the centre of town that again celebrates Provence's age-old love of aromatic plants *(see p47)*.

4 Jardin de l'Alchimiste, Eygalières

Set around a Renaissance hotel are two gardens in one. First, the Magical Plant Garden, with plants prized in Provence for their healing properties. Secondly, the Alchemist's Garden, which uses stones, water and plants to re-create symbols alchemists used in their search for the meaning of life. ✆ *Mas de la Brune • Map D4 • Open May–mid-Jun: 10am–6pm daily; mid-Jun–Sep: 10am–6pm Sat, Sun, pub hols • Reservations recommended for guided tours • DA • Adm*

5 Musée International de la Parfumerie, Grasse

Many of Provence's aromatic plants are used in the perfume industry. This museum covers perfume's 3,000-year history, from both practical and fashion angles. It includes exhibits from the Chanel fashion house and other designer names, plus Marie-Antoinette's travelling kit and a greenhouse of exotic and regional plants. Perfumes are also available for sale *(see p106)*.

Valensole Plateau

6 The second lavender-growing expanse of Provence after Sault also bursts into colour in July and August. Waves of blue and purple roll away towards the Alps, flanking the road from Riez to Digne-les-Bains. ✎ *Map C3*

Thermes, Digne-les-Bains

7 Digne is called "les Bains" (baths) because you can take the waters there. Alongside traditional medical treatments, and two thermal pools, the modern spa area offers a wide range of relaxing aromatic plant treatments. ✎ *Les Thermes • Map E2 • Open Apr–Nov: 8–11:30am, 2–5pm Mon–Fri, 8–11:30am Sat (Sep–mid-Oct: also 2–5pm); Dec–Mar: 8am–noon, 2–6pm Mon–Fri • Adm • www.thermesdignelesbains.com*

Domaines and Distilleries de Provence, Forcalquier

8 Producers of herb-based liqueurs, including a *pastis* made with more than 50 plants *(see p52)*.

Musée de la Lavande, Le Coustellet

9 The museum covers the story of lavender from field to distillery and beyond. There are 16th-century copper stills and a video explaining distillation. ✎ *276 rte de Gordes • Map B4 • Open Feb–Apr & Oct–Dec: 9am–12:15pm, 2–6pm daily; May–Sep: 9am–7pm daily • Closed Jan, 25 Dec • DA • Adm • www.museedela lavande.com*

La Ferme de Gerbaud, Lourmarin

10 The farmstead specializes in herbs, aromatic plants and plants used for dyes. Discover the entire process. ✎ *Campagne Gerbaud • Map C4 • Open Apr–Oct: 5pm tour Tue, Thu, Sat; Nov–Mar: 3pm tour Sun • Adm • www.plantes-aromatiques-provence.com*

Top 10 Aromatic Plant Products

1 Toiletries
Lavender has always been associated with hygiene, and is used for soaps, perfume and shampoo.

2 Honey
Herbs and lavender provide great pickings for bees.

3 Dried Flowers
Clonal selection has been necessary to create lavender plants whose flowers remain blue even after drying.

4 Food Flavouring
In dried or fresh form, herbs are vital ingredients of Provençal cooking *(see p51)*.

5 Essential Oils
Taken internally or applied externally, Provençal plant distillates have been part of the regional healing armoury for centuries. They need a lot of dilution – follow instructions.

6 Liqueurs
Provençal folk make many alcoholic drinks by macerating or distilling plants – not only *pastis* but also *chicouloun*, *origan de Comtat* (marjoram-based) and others.

7 Herbal Tea
Different sorts of herbal tea can relieve stress, aid digestion and improve sleep.

8 Hulled Lavender Flowers
For perfuming your wardrobe, and keeping moths out.

9 Aromatic Sticks
Once lit, depending on the essence used, the sticks will clean the atmosphere, banish odours or, in the case of citronella, keep mosquitoes away.

10 Candles
Herb-perfumed candles have a nice smell to match the soft light.

Left **Sailing** Right **Windsurfers**

📇10 Sporting Activities

Walking
From the coastal paths to mountain tracks inland, Provence could have been created for walkers. Strollers may amble around bays or along woodland paths, while serious hikers can take to the National Hiking Trails (Grandes Randonnées or GR) which criss-cross the region.

Sailing
Almost all the coastal resorts have well-equipped pleasure ports and cater for both the beginner and the experienced. The islands of Porquerolles and Bendor (see pp44–5) have renowned sailing schools.

Climbing
For some of France's finest, toughest rock climbing, head for the Buoux cliffs in the Luberon (see p117), the Verdon Gorges, with 933 routes (see pp10–11) or

Rock climbing

the creeks between Marseille and Cassis (see p66). Easier conditions can be found in the Dentelles de Montmirail (see p118).

Scuba Diving
The richness of marine life, clear waters and a sprinkling of wrecks all draw divers to the Mediterannean coast. The Iles d'Hyères are noted for their sea-scapes and for the underwater "discovery trail" on Port-Cros (see p45). Cavalaire and Marseille remain, however, the best known and best equipped centres.

Canoeing
The classic trip is to canoe down the Verdon Gorges – a two-day, turbulent, 24-km (15-mile) trip from Carrejuan Bridge to Lac de Ste-Croix (see p11). Slightly calmer spirits might prefer canoeing La Sorgue, from Fontaine-de-Vaucluse (see p118).

Skiing
Skiing is concentrated where Provence and the Alps meet. In the Ubaye valley, Pra-Loup, Le Sauze and Super-Sauze offer international-standard facilities as, in the Allos valley, do La Foux and Seignus. Meanwhile, there's family-standard skiing on Mont Ventoux – notably at Mont Serein.

Golf
The finest golfing can be found at the Frégate golf course, St Cyr, where the sea views are sensational (see p83). Other

For beach activities on the Provençal coast **See p83**

courses offering good golf in lovely surroundings include the Golf de l'Esterel at St Raphaël, the Ballesteros-designed Pont-Royal at Mallemort and Golf de Châteaublanc outside Avignon.

Mountain Biking
The marked trails, up and down mountains, through vineyards, forests, gorges and creeks, are endlessly inviting. Figanières is a key centre in the Upper Var while the Alpes de Haute-Provence has some 1,500 km (900 miles) of marked tracks.

Windsurfing

Windsurfing
Frequent winds make the Var and Bouches-du-Rhône coasts ideal for board folk. As the Mistral whistles across the Camargue, so windsurfers take advantage at Les-Saintes-Maries-de-la-Mer and Port-St-Louis (see p21).

Canyon Running
The exhilarating sport of descending torrents and canyons by abseiling, jumping and swimming has taken off big time. Try it in the Roya valley near Saorge or in any of 70 sites in the Ubaye and Verdon valleys. There are easier descents for beginners in the Pennafort and Destel gorges.

Top 10 Walks

1 Vallée des Merveilles, Mercantour National Park
Serious hikers only on this marvellous mountain trek. Allow 2–3 days, overnighting in refuges. Contact Park HQ before setting out (see p105).

2 Martel Trail, Verdon Gorges
A 15-km (9-mile) trail from Le Palud to Point Sublime. Allow 7–8 hours (see p11).

3 Calanques, Marseille
Spectacular walking along headland trails (see p66).

4 Massif des Maures
The forests, valleys and peaks are criss-crossed with excellent trails (see p83).

5 Coastal Path, Six-Fours-les-Plages
The seaside walk to La Seyne starts off flat, then climbs to the Cap Sicié. Great views. Allow 7 hours. ◊ Map D6

6 Baou de St-Jeannet, St-Jeannet
The "baou" is the rock overlooking the village near Vence. Stiff but rewarding walk (3–4 hours). ◊ Map G4

7 Port-Cros, Iles d'Hyères
A paradise of forests, creeks and headlands. Walk the coast in 5 hours (see p44).

8 Dentelles de Montmirail
Trek from Sablet village up to St Amand, the highest point. Six hours (see p118).

9 Vieux Nice
From the Old Town up to Castle Hill and down again: the best in-town walking in the region (see pp16–17).

10 Massif de l'Esterel
The best mountain path is from Pont de l'Esterel to Mont Vinaigre. Four hours (see p78).

Left & Right **Avignon Festival**

🔟 Festivals and Events

1 Avignon Festival

France's greatest theatre event is really two festivals. The official one takes over the Papal Palace's Courtyard of Honour (see p8) and other venues for modern and classical drama. But it is the unofficial "off" festival which enlivens the town, with street performers and up to 400 shows a day, from dance to burlesque comedy. ⊗ *Jul • Map B3*

2 Nice Jazz Festival

The best of the region's many jazz festivals puts on 75 concerts over eight days. World-famous names, such as BB King and Al Jarreau, show up to play in the 2,000-year-old Cimiez amphitheatre. ⊗ *Jul • Map Q3*

3 Cannes Film Festival

Some 30,000 film professionals attend the world's main cine-gathering, to do business

Gérard Depardieu, Cannes Film Festival

and, incidentally, see a few movies. The atmosphere is glamorously electric. But, as a member of the public, don't expect to meet stars, or even see them, except as they mount the stairs of the Festival Palace for a screening. ⊗ *May • Map G4*

4 Aix Festival

Since 1948, this has been a great lyrical event. As well as classical opera in the courtyard of the Archbishop's Palace, there are more contemporary works, such as Bartók and Britten, recitals and concerts by younger musicians, as well as music masterclasses at its Académie Européenne de Musique and street theatre. ⊗ *Jul • Map C4*

5 Musique en Pays de Fayence

Celebrated string quartets bring their music to the lovely Gothic, Baroque and Romanesque churches of the perched villages around Fayence. In a little-known but moving festival, the old stone buildings echo to the works of great masters. ⊗ *Late Oct/early Nov • Map F4*

6 Chorégies d'Orange

France's oldest music festival, started in 1860, has the town's Roman theatre as its main venue (see p117). The original stage wall ensures perfect acoustics for the classical operas that have earned the event an international reputation. ⊗ *Jul–early Aug • Map B2*

7 International Piano Festival, Roque d'Anthéron

Since 1980, the festival has drawn the cream of the world's classical and jazz pianists to play beneath the plane trees and night sky at the Château de Florans. ✎ *Mid-Jul–mid-Aug • Map F4*

8 Nice Carnival

Over three weeks in February, France's fifth city blows all its gaskets as multicoloured floats, grotesque carnival figures and performing troupes take to the streets. Europe's liveliest carnival also features the famous battle of the flowers. ✎ *Feb • Map H4*

Nice Carnival

9 Fête de la Véraison, Châteauneuf-du-Pape

To celebrate the ripening of their grapes, villagers dress up in medieval guise for street parades and performances and a torch-lit banquet. ✎ *1st weekend Aug • Map B3*

10 Fête de la Transhumance, St Rémy-de-Provence

Upwards of 3,000 sheep cram into the old village, for an old-style sheep drive *(transhumance)* to upland summer pastures. Along with sheep, goats and donkeys are shepherds in traditional costume, food displays and feasting. ✎ *Whitsun weekend • Map B3*

Top 10 Sporting Events

1 Monaco Grand Prix

The jet-set come together for the only street race on the Formula One calendar. ✎ *May • Map H3*

2 Les Voiles de St-Tropez

Six-day regatta for both traditional and modern sailing boats. ✎ *Sep–Oct • Map F5*

3 Pétanque World Championships, Marseille

Four days of *boules*, culminating in a final on the Vieux Port. ✎ *Jul • Map K4*

4 Olympic Sailing Week, Hyères

Some 1,000 boats from 50 nations compete in this sailing event. ✎ *Apr • Map F6*

5 Feria du Riz, Arles

Bullfighting and festivities to welcome the Camargue rice harvest. ✎ *Sep • Map B4*

6 Beach Volleyball World Series, Marseille

The French leg of the World Volleyball Grand Slam, and the richest. ✎ *Jul • Map C5*

7 Monte Carlo Tennis Masters

One of the tennis circuit's more prestigious events. ✎ *Apr • Map H3*

8 Olympique de Marseille

The favourite French football team *(see p66)* plays home games July to May.

9 Joûtes Provencales, St Mandrier-sur-Mer

An interested sporting event of waterborne jousting. ✎ *Jul–Aug • Map G4*

10 Verdon Canyon Challenge

Punishing races of 8–100 km (5–62 miles) through this dramatic scenery. ✎ *Jun • Map E3*

Left **Château d'If** Right **Pénitents des Mées**

Provençal Legends

1 Saintes-Maries-de-la-Mer
After being set adrift in a boat from Palestine, Mary Jacoby (sister of the Virgin), Mary Salome, Mary Magdalene, Lazarus and servant girl, Sara landed on the Provençal coast. They were the first Christians in Gaul. The "relics" of Jacoby and Salome are found in the town's church, as are those of Sara, patron saint of gypsies *(see p74)*.

2 Man in the Iron Mask
Who was the Man in the Iron Mask? Louis XIV's troublesome brother? A meddling royal priest? No one knows. Certainly, he was dangerous enough to be clamped in the mask and locked away in Château d'If from 1687. You may visit the island fort and see his cell *(see p69)*. ✎ Map G4

3 Vallée des Merveilles, Mercantour National Park
Almost 4,000 years ago Ligurian tribespeople covered rocks in the Alpine valley with engravings – theories abound about their meaning. The site is superb but difficult to access *(see p105)*.

4 Les Pénitents des Mées
In AD 800 a congregation of monks ogled female Saracen prisoners being led to the River Durance and were turned to stone as punishment. There they remain – a 2-km (1-mile) line of rocks, some 100 m (300 ft) high, looking like repentant monks with their cowls up *(see p114)*.

5 Pont d'Avignon
In 1177 a shepherd boy named Bénézet received orders from God that a bridge should be built across the Rhône. Avignon people were sceptical, so the lad picked up a rock which 30 strong men couldn't shift and carried it to where Pont St-Bénézet was to begin *(see p122)*.

6 La Tarasque, Tarascon
Tarasque, a dragon-like beast, terrorized Tarascon in the 1st century AD, until St Martha sprinkled it with Holy Water. Tarascon converted to Christianity *(see p73)* and Tarasque remains central to the town's June festival.

7 St Maximin-de-la-Ste-Baume
After landing in Provence, Mary Magdalene spread the Christian word, before spending her last

Tarascon

St Maximin-de-la-Ste-Baume basilica

years praying in a cave in the Ste-Baume mountains. Her remains were discovered in the 13th century and may be seen in the Gothic basilica *(see p78)*.

Lost "City of God"
The Latin inscription on a rock near St-Geniez indicates the site of a 5th-century "Theopolis", or City of God Christian centre. The rock aside, no trace has been found. However, phenomena including strange lights and odd weather add to the mystery of the place. ✎ *Map G3*

Roussillon
The red cliffs of Roussillon are not coloured by accident. In medieval times the local lord's wife, Sirmonde, fell in love with a troubadour. The lord had him killed and Sirmonde threw herself off a cliff, staining the rocks with her blood *(see p123)*.

Cathérine Ségurane, Nice
Washerwoman Cathérine led Niçois resistance against the Turkish fleet that besieged the city in 1543. She knocked out the Turkish standard-bearer with her washboard, before lifting her skirts and putting the rest of the Turks to flight. The day was eventually lost, but Cathérine's statue is in Vieux Nice *(see pp16–17)*.

Top 10 Traditions

1 Midnight Mass, Christmas Eve
Pastoral memories mix with Christian ritual, as live lambs participate in the ceremony.

2 Thirteen Christmas Desserts
Symbolizing Christ and the Apostles, the climax of the Christmas Eve meal includes dried fruit and griddle cakes.

3 Nativity Scene
Scenes mix biblical characters with *santon* figures of Provençal villagers *(see p134)*.

4 Fête de la St-Jean
In Valréas medieval parades attend the election of a boy-child to "protect" the town. ✎ *Map G4 • 23 Jun*

5 Fête des Tripettes, Barjols
Incongruously, celebrates both the relics of St Marcel and the importance of bulls.
✎ *Map E5 • 2nd weekend Jan*

6 Fête de la Tarasque, Tarascon
Tarasque "reappears" to terrify revellers. ✎ *Map B3*
• Last weekend Jun

7 Fête de la Transhumance, Riez
Sheep cross the village to upland pasture, giving rise to festivities. ✎ *Map E3*
• Sun, mid-Jun

8 Fête de la Lavande, Sault
The heartland of lavender *(see p54)* celebrates its traditions.
✎ *Map D3 • 15 Aug*

9 Fête des Mimosas, Bormes-les-Mimosas
Festivities amid the flowers *(see p78)*. ✎ *Map E5 • Mid-Feb*

10 Fête des Vins, Bandol
The wine district welcomes the new vintage.
✎ *Map D5 • 1st Sun, Dec*

AROUND PROVENCE

PROVENCE'S TOP 10

Left **Fort St Nicholas** Right **Marseille harbour**

Marseille

THE OLDEST CITY IN FRANCE *was founded 2,600 years ago by Greek set-tlers from Asia Minor, and it has barely seen a quiet moment since. Open-hearted and tumultuous, it is backed by chalk hills and flanked by white cliffs, with its face to the sea. The sea is Marseille's raison d'être, making it a trad-ing hub and entry point for immigrants. As a result, Marseille is a collection of urban villages, from the souk-like market areas to tiny fishing settlements. But all the inhabitants are Marseillais: loud, rebellious and volatile. This is the home of French music, football and bouillabaisse, the most flavoursome fish dish in the world. Picaresque and picturesque, it's a place in which to feel alive.*

🔟 Sights

1. Vieux Port
2. Notre-Dame-de-la-Garde
3. Le Panier and Vieille Charité
4. Palais Longchamp
5. Musée Grobet-Labadié
6. Les Calanques
7. Prado Beaches
8. Fort St-Nicholas
9. Château d'If
10. Musée des Arts Décoratifs, de la Faïence et de la Mode

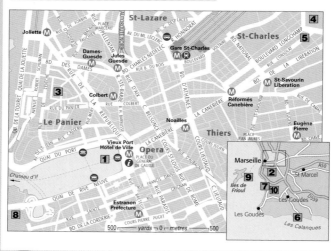

Vieux Port

Commercial sea traffic might have moved round the corner to newer docks in the 19th century, but the old port remains the heart of city life. Bobbing with pleasure boats and fringed with restaurants, it's where the *Marseillais* gather for festivities and to buy fish at the market. The occupying Germans attempted to subdue the city by blowing up the port's north side in 1943, but Marseille's indomitable nature won the day. ◈ *Map K4*

Notre-Dame-de-la-Garde

This Romanesque-Byzantine church is the symbol of Marseille. Perched on the city's highest hill and topped by a great, gold statue of the Virgin, it can be seen from everywhere in the city and is itself all-seeing: the views from the church are spectacular. Built in the 1850s and restored in the early 2000s, the vaulted crypt is carved out of the rock, while the sanctuary is rich with mosaics and marble. ◈ *Rue Forte du Sanctuaire • Map K6 • Open 7am–6:30pm daily (7:30pm Jun–Sep) • Free*

Le Panier and Vieille Charité

Wriggling up the hill to the north of the Vieux Port, Le Panier is Marseille's oldest sector. This is where the Greeks settled and, in

Notre-Dame-de-la-Garde

subsequent centuries, where the city's immigrants began their new lives. They still do – the tiny streets are alive with different accents and cultures. The main feature is La Vieille Charité, the 17th-century workhouse now transformed into a wonderful cultural centre. It houses the museums of Mediterranean Archaeology and of African, Oceanic and Native American Art. Especially noteworthy is the domed central chapel – Italian Baroque at its purest. ◈ *Map J3 • La Vieille Charité: 2 rue de la Charité, Open 10am–6pm Tue–Sun; Closed 1 Jan, 1 May, 1 Nov, 25 Dec • DA • Adm*

Palais Longchamp

Longchamp is the greatest expression of Marseille's 19th-century "golden age". What is essentially a water tower is embellished in palatial Second Empire style. Fountains, columns and animal sculptures evoke abundance and fertility. The central gallery is flanked by two ornate wings, home to the Fine Arts and Natural History museums. Lush gardens stretch behind. ◈ *6 blvd de Montricher • Map M3 • Museums: Open 10am–5pm Tue–Sun; Closed pub hols, Adm (free Sun)*

Palais Longchamp

City Pass *gives one- to three-day access to museums and public transport at substantial savings. Contact the tourist office (see p130).*

Les Calanques

Musée Grobet-Labadié

Situated opposite the Palais Longchamp, this museum is set in the former private mansion of a 19th-century rich, art-loving Marseille family. Its original decor has been carefully retained, recreating bourgeois life at the peak of the city's prosperity. If the house itself is elegant and sober, the art collection is wonderfully eclectic. Walls are decorated with a unique collection of Gobelin and Aubusson tapestries, while the 10 different salons boast an overwhelming abundance of sculpture, paintings, drawings and furniture from the 13th to 19th centuries, and much more besides. All in all, a discreetly sensual delight. ◈ 140 blvd Longchamp • Map M3 • Open 10am–6pm Tue–Sun • Adm

---

The Football Capital

First champions of Europe, then enmeshed in match-fixing scandals, the recent history of the Olympique de Marseille football team has matched the turbulence of its home town. But this has done nothing to dissuade the fans of the most popular French team – football is the life blood of Marseille life, the Stade Vélodrome its place of worship.

Les Calanques

Within 15 minutes' drive of Marseille's centre, you are out of the city and into a different world. Here white rocks plunge into the blue sea and the road snakes into inlets (calanques) of great beauty, and small settlements. This is where the Marseillais spend their weekends, eating, drinking and keeping rich developers out. After the "village" of Les Goudes, the road peters out and access to other, even more picturesque creeks (towards Cassis) is by foot or boat (see p42). ◈ Map C5

Prado Beaches

Around the corniche from the Vieux Port and past the tiny, picturesque fishing port of Vallon des Auffes stretch Marseille's resolutely modern beaches. They were reclaimed from the sea with earth excavated during the construction of the city's metro system. Now they run round to the start of the calanques. On summer days, they throb with every conceivable beach sporting activity; at night, the Escale Borély beach area offers some of the town's trendiest nightspots (see p69). ◈ Map C5

Fort St-Nicholas

On the south side of the Vieux Port is Marseille's fort, built in 1680 by Louis XIV to impose authority on the truculent city – its cannons pointed inland. Star-shaped and built on two levels in pink-tinged limestone, it stares across at the much older St Jean fort. Now split in two by the 19th-century port-side boulevard, St-Nicholas remains one of the city's most imposing buildings. ◈ Blvd Charles Livron • Map J5

9 Château d'If

This offshore island fortress was built in the 16th century to protect the city's port and was turned into a prison in 1634. Among its inmates were the real Comte de Mirabeau, and the fictional Count of Monte Cristo, the antihero of Alexander Dumas' novel of the same name *(see p37)*. The fortress is accessible by ferry from the Vieux Port. ◈ *Map C5 • Open Apr–Aug: 9:30am–6:30pm daily; Sep–Mar: 9am–5:30pm Tue–Sun • Adm*

10 Musée des Arts Décoratifs, de la Faïence et de la Mode

Fully restored to its former glory, Château Borély, a masterpiece of 18th-century architecture, now houses exhibition space devoted to three genres: decorative arts and furniture; earthenware, ceramics and glass; and fashion from the 17th century to the present day. The museum brings together collections formerly scattered between the Musée de la Faïence, Musée Cantini and the Musée de Vieux Marseille, along with the furniture collection of the Château itself. The lovely gardens also host outdoor exhibitions and concerts. ◈ *Château Borély, 134 ave Clôt Bey • Map C5 • Open 10am–6pm Tue–Sun • Closed 1 Jan, 1 May, 1 Nov, 25 Dec • DA*

Château d'If

A morning exploring Marseille

From the Quai des Belges on the **Vieux Port** *(see p65)* walk up La Canebière, the commercial hub of the 19th-century city, where you can still sense the Second Empire grandeur. Almost immediately on the left, the Palais de la Bourse (Stock Exchange) is a monumental expression of trading confidence; it now contains the Musée de la Marine detailing Marseille's sea-going history *(Open daily • Adm)*. At the Neo-Gothic Eglise des Réformés, cross to place Stalingrad and enjoy a drink by the fountain at Brasserie Danaïdes.

Take the leafy cours Joseph Thierry, then blvd Longchamp to the **Musée Grobet-Labadié** and **Palais Longchamp** *(see p65)*, then wander the lush Longchamp park to place Maréchal Foch. Take the blvd de la Libération, left into rue St Savournin to cours Julien, a lively centre for musicians and artists.

Wriggle down to the place du Marché des Capucins, heart of the city's *souk* market area, then up the style with the designer shops of rue St Ferréol.

Turn right onto rue Grignan to visit the **Musée Cantini** *(Open 10am–6pm Tue–Sun • Closed pub hols • Adm)*, which houses a magnificent Modernist collection of Fauvist, Cubist and Surrealist paintings.

End your morning stroll at place Thiars, a hive of galleries, restaurants and bars. You will have more than deserved your lunch at **Le Caribou** *(see p69)*.

Left **Faïencerie Figuères** Right **Four des Navettes**

🔟 Specialist Shops

1 G Bataille
Finest grocery-cum-delicatessen in Marseille, with irresistible selections of cheese, cold meats, spices, wines and much else besides. 🏬 *25 pl Notre-Dame-du-Mont • Map L4*

2 Rue de la Tour
Not one shop but the tiny street where some of Marseille's leading fashion creators congregate, among them Manon Martin, Zenane and Casablanca. 🏬 *Map K4*

3 Faïencerie Figuères
Extraordinary enamelled terracotta figures of fruit, vegetables and meat. Artisan works that look good enough to eat. 🏬 *10–12 ave Lauzier • Map C5 • Closed mid-Aug–mid-Sep • www.faiencerie-figueres.com*

4 Boutique de la Compagnie de Provence-Marseille
Not far from the Vieux Port, this shop sells authentic olive-oil *savon de Marseille* in all its forms. 🏬 *1 rue Caisserie • Map J4*

5 Casablanca
One of the arbiters of trendy Marseille style, featuring colourful, easy-to-wear women's clothing. 🏬 *63 cours Julien • Map L4*

6 La Chocolatière de Panier
This tiny establishment makes the best chocolate in the city. Specialities include the delicious *Barre Marseillaise*, stuffed with candied fruits and nuts. 🏬 *49 rue de Petit Puits • Map J3*

7 Nouvelles Galeries
The largest store in town is the one-stop shop (clothes, gifts, wines, groceries and more) for those with less time to spare. 🏬 *Centre Commercial Bourse • Map K3*

8 La Part des Anges
Not only a good wine shop and delicatessen but also a restaurant and sophisticated take-away outlet. In addition, it's open every night until 2am. 🏬 *33 rue Sainte • Map J5*

9 Le Four des Navettes
The oldest bakery in town and, since 1781, home of the traditional Marseillais *navette*, a small biscuit (cookie) flavoured with orange blossom and, aptly for this port city, shaped like a boat. 🏬 *136 rue Sainte • Map J5*

10 Dromel Aîné
Even older than the above, Dromel Aîné has been in the business of selling fantastic chocolates, sweets, and a range of unusual teas and coffees since 1760. An unmissable Marseille experience. 🏬 *19 ave Prado • Map L6*

Around Provence – Marseille

Price Categories

For a three-course meal for one with half a bottle of wine (or equivalent meal), taxes and extra charges.	€ under €30
	€€ €30–€40
	€€€ €40–€50
	€€€€ €50–€60
	€€€€€ over €60

Above **Chez Madie Les Galinettes**

🔟 Places to Eat

Restaurant Chez Michel
Known for serving the finest *bouillabaisse* in town, as well as other traditional Marseillaise seafood specialities. Overlooks Catalan beach. ✎ *6 rue des Catalans • Map J4 • 04 91 52 30 63 • DA • €€€*

Chez Madie Les Galinettes
Exceptional Provençal dishes such as *pieds et paquets* and *daube (see p51)*. Local painters are exhibited inside. ✎ *138 quai du Port • Map J4 • 04 91 90 40 87 • Closed Sat L in summer, Sun • €*

Chez Toinou
One of the best – and cheapest – places for seafood in Marseille. Adventurous sorts can savour a *plateau de fruits de mer* for about €15; for more traditional types, there's mussels and chips. ✎ *3 cours St Louis • Map L4 • 08 11 45 45 45 • Closed Sun, Mon • DA • €€€*

Les Arcenaulx
Extraordinary vaulted setting in the former 17th-century arsenal. Besides the regional restaurant, there is a bookshop, a boutique and an air of mystery. ✎ *25 cours d'Estienne d'Orves • Map K5 • 04 91 59 80 30 • Closed Sun • €€€*

La Table du Fort
A welcoming husband-and-wife team consistently serve inventive modern cuisine using local produce, just a few steps from the Vieux Port. ✎ *8 rue Fort Notre Dame • Map K5 • 04 91 33 97 65 • Closed Sun, Sat–Mon L • €€€*

Le Souk
Great Moroccan food, in a lovely setting with a view of the cathedral. ✎ *Quai du Port • Map J4 • 04 91 91 29 29 • Closed Mon • DA • €€€*

L'Epuisette
Set amid Marseille's traditional seaside cabins, L'Epuisette has its feet in the water but its mind firmly on fresh fish. ✎ *Vallon des Auffes • Map C5 • 04 91 52 17 82 • Closed Sun, Mon • €€€€*

29 Place aux Huiles
Dishes change with the seasons here, but there is always something interesting on the menu. ✎ *29 place aux Huiles • Map K5 • 04 91 33 26 44 • Closed Sun D • €€€€*

Les Trois Forts
Great views over the port to accompany fine regional cuisine. ✎ *Hôtel Sofitel du Vieux-Port, 36 blvd Charles-Livon • Map C5 • 04 91 15 59 56 • DA • €€€€*

Le Caribou
First-rate fish and game has been served here since 1945. ✎ *38 pl Thiars • Map K5 • 06 74 90 57 64 • Closed Sun, Mon, Jun–Sep • DA • €€€€*

Note: *Unless otherwise stated, all restaurants accept credit cards and serve vegetarian meals*

Left **Bouches-du-Rhône landscape** Right **Barbentane château, near Tarascon**

Bouches-du-Rhône

THE BOUCHES-DU-RHÔNE REGION IS WELL NAMED (bouches *means mouths*), for here the broad channel of France's most important river splits into several separate streams, flowing into the Mediterranean via lagoons and grassy plains. This is the Camargue, a unique wetland partly protected by conservation areas. The Rhône is Provence's western boundary and for centuries the river was the region's highway. Hence, some of its most important towns grew up along its banks, while villages and medieval abbeys are tucked away in the hills. On the coast, windswept beaches fringe the Camargue, but east of the delta the landscape becomes rocky, with many small inlets (calanques).

🔟 Sights

1. Roman Arles
2. Aix-en-Provence
3. The Camargue
4. St-Rémy-de-Provence and Glanum
5. Les-Baux-de-Provence
6. Abbaye de Montmajour
7. Abbaye de Silvacane
8. Cassis
9. Château du Tarascon
10. Salon de Provence

Cours Mirabeau, Aix

1 Roman Arles

The delightful town of Arles, founded by the Romans, stands on the east bank of the Rhône and is the gateway to Provence from the west *(see pp12–13)*.

2 Aix-en-Provence

Aix is just a stone's throw from the sprawl of Marseille, but keeps its own identity, with cosmopolitan cafés, a grand cathedral and beautiful 18th-century fountains *(see pp14–15)*.

3 The Camargue

This vast expanse of salt marshes, lagoons and grazing land, home to rare bird and animals species, is protected within the Parc Naturel Régional de Camargue and other conservation areas *(see pp20–21)*.

4 St Rémy-de-Provence and Glanum

Overlooked by Les Alpilles, a thickly wooded, miniature sierra of limestone hills, St-Rémy is a perfect exploring base. Mansions built during the 15th and 16th centuries grace its historic centre. One of them was the original home of the de Sade family, ancestors of the notorious Marquis, and now houses the small Musée des Alpilles, displaying Roman artifacts that were found at Glanum, about 30 minutes' walk from the town centre. Here, the site of one of the most ancient Greek-Roman

Herbs, St-Rémy-de-Provence

settlements in Provence is landmarked by a magnificent triumphal arch and mausoleum, known collectively as Les Antiques *(see p30)*. ✎ Map B3
• *Musée des Alpilles: pl Favier, St-Rémy; Open Jun–Sep: 10am–6pm Tue–Sun; Oct–May: 1–5:30pm Tue–Sat; Closed 1 Jan, 1 May, 25 Dec; Adm*

5 Les-Baux-de-Provence

Perched on a limestone crag, Les Baux is one of Provence's most dramatic fortified villages. It is crowned by a ruined citadel, the Château des Baux, whose walls date from the 10th century. Eglise St-Vincent has 20th-century stained-glass windows by Max Ingrand. The village is closed to cars *(see p38)*. ✎ Map B4 • *Château des Baux: Open daily. Apr–Jun & Sep: 9am–7:15pm; Jul & Aug: 9am–8:15pm; Nov–Feb: 10am–5pm; Adm*

Les-Baux-de-Provence

Left **Abbaye de Silvacane** Right **Market, Aix-en-Provence**

Abbaye de Montmajour

This massive, fortress-like abbey, built by Benedictine monks in the 10th century, can be seen from a great distance. When it was built, the low hill on which it now stands was an island surrounded by pools and marshes and is still, appropriately, known as Mount Ararat. Damaged by fire in 1726, the abbey was restored during the 19th century, and its Eglise Notre-Dame is one of the largest Romanesque buildings in Provence. Below the church, a 12th-century crypt and chapel have been carved into the hillside *(see p32).* ✪ *Rte de Fontvieille, Arles • Map B4 • Open Apr–Jun: 9:30am–6pm daily; Jul–Sep: 10am–6:30pm daily; Oct–Mar: 10am–5pm Tue–Sun • Closed 1 Jan, 1 May, 1 & 11 Nov, 25 Dec • Adm*

Abbaye de Silvacane

Along with Sénanque *(see pp24–5)* and Thoronet, Silvacane is one of the three great sister-abbeys constructed in the 12th century by the Cistercian order as it rose to prominence in Provence. Its plain, austere architecture

---

Black Bulls and White Horses

The wild black *taureaux* (bulls) of the Camargue are one of the symbols of Bouches-du-Rhône, along with the sturdy white horses – direct descendants of the prehistoric wild horse of Europe. These are still ridden by the *gardians*, the sombrero-wearing cowboys of the Camargue pastures.

---

reflects the rule of the order, which was founded by St Bernard in protest at the luxury and corruption of other monasteries. The church has a high, vaulted transept and the cloister arcades and refectory were added in the 13th and 14th centuries. Abandoned by its monks in the late 14th century, it became a living abbey once again in the 20th century. ✪ *La Roque d'Anthéron • Map C4 • Open Jun–Sep: 10am–6pm daily; Oct–May: 10am–1pm, 2–5pm Tue–Sun • Adm*

Cassis

This delightfully pretty fishing port *(see p39)* with its brightly coloured fishing boats anchored in a harbour on a rugged, rocky coastline, was a favourite with painters such as Dufy, Derain and Matisse *(see pp36–7)*, all of whom were inspired by its clear light and bright Mediterranean hues. Amazingly, it has escaped being spoiled by tourism, and there are pretty rocky coves *(calanques)* and beaches nearby. Cassis is also noted for its excellent seafood (fresh sea urchins are considered a local delicacy) and there are plenty of good restaurants. ✪ *Map D5*

Château de Tarascon

The white battlements of the Château de Tarascon seem straight from a historical romance. Built to guard a vital crossing of the Rhône on Provence's borders, the riverside castle has steep, crenellated curtain walls between massive round towers and looks impregnable. It was begun by King Louis of Anjou, ruler of Provence in the 15th century, and was completed by his successor, King René. On his death, Provence became part of France *(see p29)* and the castle lost its strategic importance, be-coming a prison until 1926 *(see p60)*. 🗺 *Blvd du Roi René, Tarascon • Map B3 • Open Feb–May & Oct: 9:30am–5:30pm daily; Jun–Sep: 9:30am–6:30pm daily; Nov–Jan: 9:30am–5pm daily • Closed public hols • Adm*

🔟 Salon de Provence

Salon, one of the oldest villages in Provence, is today a busy modern town, host to the French Air Force training school. The old town, sitting on a hill, has an attractive historic centre, with medieval buildings, quiet streets and leafy, café-lined squares. The main attraction is the Chateau de l'Empéri *(see p74)* dating from the 10th century. Other places to visit include the small museum dedicated to Nostradamus, who lived here in the 16th century, and the Musée de Savon at Savonnerie Fabre, which bears witness to the olive oil industry which has existed here for over 600 years. 🗺 *Map B4*

Château de Tarascon

Little Rome: A Morning in Arles

Start the day with a visit to the largest and most striking Roman monument in Provence, **Les Arènes** *(see p12)*. From the highest tier of seats you have a fine view of the historic centre and the Rhône. From here, walk across to the **Théâtre Antique** *(see p12)*, for another glimpse of Roman Arles, then walk down the rue du Cloître to the place de la République, where water gushes from bronze masks at the foot of an obelisk, brought here from Egypt by the Romans.

On the east side of the square, visit the fine Romanesque **Eglise St-Trophime** *(see p12)*, with its lovely sculpted pillars crowned by little figures of saints and martyrs. Follow the rue de l'Hôtel de Ville to **Les Thermes de Constantin** *(see p12)*, the remains of a palace built for a 4th-century AD Roman emperor. Then spend up to an hour in the Musée Réattu *(Rue du Grand-Prieuré • Open Tue–Sun • Adm)*, with its fine collection of 18th–20th-century art, including works by Picasso.

Another great painter, Van Gogh, is associated with place du Forum, cluttered with cafés – one has been painted to look just as it was in his work *Café la Nuit*. Stop in for coffee. End the morning at the Museon Arlaten *(Rue de la Républi-que • Closed for renovation until 2015)*, where the largest folklore collection in Provence vividly recalls some of the region's rich and fading traditions *(see pp60–61)*.

Left **Ceiling, Abbaye de St-Michel de Frigolet** Right **Doll's carriage, Château de Barbentane**

10 Best of the Rest

1 Centre de Ginès and Parc Ornithologique du Pont-de-Gau, Camargue

For a spectacular view of the Camargue, visit the bird park, where enclosures display the lagoons' bird life *(see p20)*. ✆ *Map B5 • Open 9am–6pm daily (10am–5pm Oct–Mar) • Adm*

2 Musée de la Camargue, The Camargue

The Camargue comes to life in this fascinating museum, housed in a farmhouse *(see p20)*. ✆ *Mas du Pont de Rousty, Arles • Map B5 • Open Apr–Sep: 9am–12:30pm, 1–6pm Wed–Mon; Oct–Mar: 10am–12:30pm, 1–5pm Wed–Mon • Closed Jan, 1 May, 25 Dec • Adm*

3 Château de Barbentane

This Italianate mansion built in 1674 is ornately decorated with 17th-century antiques. ✆ *Map B3 • Open Easter–early Nov: 9am–noon, 2–6pm Thu–Tue (daily Jul–Sep) • Adm*

4 Notre-Dame des Saintes-Maries-de-la-Mer

Dominating the seaside village, this 12th-century church *(see p32)* houses relics of St Sarah and has superb views from its roof terrace. ✆ *Pl de l'Eglise • Map B5 • Open 3–6pm daily (Dec–Mar: Sat & Sun only) • Adm*

5 Eyguières

This village was the source of Arles's water supply in Roman times, via an aqueduct. A 12th-century chapel, a 17th-century church and a ruined castle stand in the village. ✆ *Map B4*

6 Château de l'Emperi, Salon-de-Provence

This imposing chateau was once the seat of the archbishops of Arles. It now houses a collection of military uniforms. ✆ *Montée du Puech • Map B4 • Open Easter–Sep: 9:30am–noon, 2–6pm Tue–Sun; Oct–Easter: 1:30–6pm Tue–Sun • Closed pub hols • Adm*

7 Abbaye de St-Michel de Frigolet

The most attractive aspect of this 19th-century abbey is its painted depictions of saints. ✆ *Map B3 • Open 8–11am, 2–6pm daily • Adm*

8 Château de Beaucaire

Facing the Château de Tarascon *(see p72)* is this ruined 11th-century chateau. ✆ *Pl Raymond VII • Map B3 • Open 10am–6pm Wed–Mon (to 5:15pm Nov–Mar) • Adm*

9 Abbaye de St-Roman

This remarkable 5th-century abbey is the only troglodyte monastery in Europe. ✆ *Map B3 • Open Apr–Jun, Sep–mid-Oct: 10am–1pm, 2–6:30pm Tue–Sun; Jul, Aug: 10am–1pm, 2–7pm daily; mid-Oct–Mar: 2–5:30pm Tue–Sun (Mar: to 6:30pm) • Closed 25 Dec • Adm*

10 Musée du Riz, Sambuc

This rice museum sits in the midst of the Camargue paddy fields. Guided tours finish with a tasting of a dish made using the local rice. ✆ *Rizerie du Petit Manusclat • Map B4 • Open 9am–12:30pm, 2–6pm Tue (Jul, Aug: Tue & Thu) • Other days & Dec–Feb by prior arrangement • Adm*

Price Categories

For a three-course meal for one with half a bottle of wine (or equivalent meal), taxes and extra charges.

€	under €30
€€	€30–€40
€€€	€40–€50
€€€€	€50–€60
€€€€€	over €60

Above **Le Garage, Martigues**

🏠10 Places to Eat

1 Le Clos de la Violette, Aix-en-Provence
Chef Jean-Marc Banzo uses the best Provençal ingredients to create memorable dishes *(see p50)*. ◈ 10 ave Violette • Map C4 • 04 42 23 30 71 • Closed Sun, Mon, 2 wks Aug • €€€€€

2 La Bastide du Cours, Aix-en-Provence
Slow-roasted lamb is one of the treats at this terracotta-toned hotel-restaurant. ◈ 43 cours Mirabeau • Map D4 • 04 42 26 10 06 • €€€€

3 Alain Assaud, Saint-Rémy-de-Provence
Delicious desserts from Monsieur Assaud, a former pastry chef now renowned for his innovative regional cuisine. ◈ 13 blvd Marceau • Map B3 • 04 90 92 37 11 • Closed Sat L in high season; Wed, Thu L, Sat L in low season; mid-Nov–mid-Mar • DA • €€€€€

4 Le Mazet du Vaccarès, Arles
Located on the edge of the Étang de Vaccarès, this is the place to sample Camargue clams in lemon cream. Open from Friday lunch to Sunday lunch. ◈ D37, route Albaron Villeneuve • Map B4 • 04 90 97 10 79 • Closed mid-Jan–Feb • No credit cards • No veg options • DA • €€€

5 Le Cilantro, Arles
Inventive modern cuisine is served in an elegant setting, with a lovely terrace for summer dining. ◈ 31 rue Port de Laure • Map B4 • 04 90 18 25 05 • Closed Sat L, Sun, Mon, 1 wk Feb • DA • €€€€€

6 La Chassagnette, Arles
Organic vegetables from the old farm's garden are made into delicious, regional dishes by chef Armand Arnal. Pick your own herbs for a digestive *tisane* at the end of the meal. ◈ Route du Sambuc • Map B4 • 04 90 97 26 96 • Closed Tue, Wed, mid-Dec–Mar • DA • €€€€€

7 L'Amphytrion, Aix-en-Provence
This place is noted equally for its wine list as its menu, which features favourites such as Sisteron lamb. ◈ 2 rue Paul Doumer • Map C4 • 04 42 26 54 10 • Closed Sun, Mon • No veg options • DA • €€

8 El Campo, Saintes-Maries-de-la-Mer
Wash down a bull-meat casserole with a glass of Costières de Nîmes while listening to live gypsy flamenco. ◈ 13 rue Victor Hugo • Map A4 • 04 90 97 84 11 • Closed Sun D, Mon, Feb–early Mar • No veg options • DA • €€

9 Villa Regalido, Fontvieille
Gastronomic restaurant using local seafood and Provençal ingredients, such as herbs. ◈ Rue Mistral • Map B4 • 04 90 54 60 22 • Closed Mon, Tue, Thu L, Jan–mid-Feb • €€€€€

10 Le Garage, Martigues
Chef Fabien Morreale cooks refined fusion dishes in an Art Deco garage. ◈ 20 ave Frédéric Mistral • Map C5 • 04 42 44 09 51 • Closed Sun, Mon, Aug, 2 wks Jan • DA • €€€€

Note: Unless otherwise stated, all restaurants accept credit cards and serve vegetarian meals

Left **Massif de l'Esterel** Centre **Cathedral, Fréjus** Right **Bas-relief, Basilica St-Maximin**

The Var and Provençal Coast

WITHIN A 30-MINUTE DRIVE OF THE GLAMOUR *of St-Tropez, you can be on a rugged mountainside so remote that you dread nightfall. That's the charm of the Var – an intoxicating mix of the easy life and a harsh landscape. In the Verdon gorges and Upper Var, nature is both wild and imposing; down below, beauty assumes more rounded forms in beach resorts and casinos. Yet the Provençal tendency to "let time take its time" unites the region. Little wonder that this is the most popular of French holiday regions.*

🔟 Sights

1. Abbaye du Thoronet, Le Thoronet
2. Sanary-sur-Mer Harbour
3. Fréjus Old Town
4. Massif d'Esterel
5. Port Grimaud
6. Place des Lices, St-Tropez
7. Basilica St-Maximim, St-Maximim-la-St-Baume
8. Bormes-les-Mimosas
9. The Caves, Villecroze
10. Musée des Traditions Provençales, Draguignan

St-Tropez old town

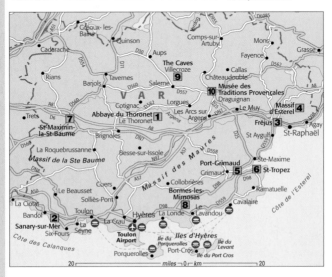

1 Abbaye du Thoronet, Le Thoronet

This majestic 12th-century Cistercian abbey was built in a wooded dip near Lorgues. Probably the finest example of Romanesque architecture in the region, along with its sister houses, Silvacane and Sénanque *(see pp24–5)*, it rises with sober magnificence. The un-mortared stones of the church, monks' buildings and cloisters are decorated only by changing sunlight, their interior volumes inspiring awe and serenity. The harmony of structure and setting make contemplation unavoidable.
Quai Abbaye • Map E4 • Open 10am–6:30pm Mon–Sat; 10am–noon, 2–6:30pm Sun (Oct–Mar: 10am–1pm, 2–5pm Mon–Sat, 10am–noon, 2–5pm Sun) • Closed 1 Jan, 1 May, 1 & 11 Nov, 25 Dec • Adm

Abbaye du Thoronet

2 Sanary-sur-Mer Harbour

The prettiest harbour in the Var remains a proper fishing port, bobbing with boats. Beyond, palm trees fringe a frontage of pastel façades. Activity varies from relaxed to intense, notably during the morning market which enlivens the Allées d'Estienne-d'Orves. The beach is nearby. So, too, are plaques commemorating Thomas Mann, Bertolt Brecht and other German writers who took refuge from the Nazis here in the 1930s. Map D5

3 Fréjus Old Town

Despite its relaxed beach bag and flip-flop image, the town of Fréjus has an exceptional double heritage. As Forum Julii, it was the second port of the Roman Empire in the region and retains some of the oldest and most extensive ancient remains in Provence. Particularly notable are the elliptical, 12,000-seater arena and theatre *(see p30)*. Meanwhile, the town's medieval bishopric status has left it with an extraordinary group of episcopal buildings. The 12th-century cathedral incorporates a wonderful octagonal baptistry from an earlier, 5th-century church, while the 14th-century cloisters have ceilings painted with bracingly lurid events from the Apocalypse *(see p32)*. A must if in the region. Map F5 • Cathédrale St-Lenoncé: • Open 9am–6:30pm daily (Oct–May: 9am–noon, 2–5pm Tue–Sun) • Closed 1 Jan, 1 May, 1 & 11 Nov, 25 Dec • Adm (cloisters only)

Harbour, Sanary-sur-Mer

Cloisters, Basilica St-Maximin

Massif de l'Esterel

As the rugged red rocks of the Esterel range plunge into the blue of the Mediterranean, they create creeks and contrasts of stirring beauty. Inland, the tough, volcanic mountains may rise no higher than 600 m (2,000 ft) but the landscape is of breathtaking gorges, passes and peaks. Many paths and tracks provide access to the mountainscape and its rich tree life. Take the Perthus or tougher Mal-Infernet valleys – in the footsteps of brigands who hid out here *(see p57)*. ☊ *Map G4*

Port Grimaud

Built in the mid-1960s over former marshland, the port is reminiscent of Venice, as brightly painted houses push out onto quays separated by canals but

---

Perched Villages

The Var's *villages perchés* were built as a defence against Saracen pirates. In the 9th century Saracens occupied parts of the Var, notably around La Garde Freinet. Expelled in 973, they returned to wreak havoc at frequent intervals up until the 18th century. The locals therefore took to the hills as a form of protection.

---

joined by little bridges. Access is by boat or by foot. Although now weathered and wearing a real Provençal look, traditionalists still prefer medieval Grimaud, perched 5 km (3 miles) inland. ☊ *Map F5*

Place des Lices, St-Tropez

Generations of artists, stars and beautiful people have made this village square possibly the best known in the world. But it remains just that – the rich and famous may come and go, but the Tuesday and Saturday markets are always here *(see p18)*. ☊ *Map F5*

Basilica St-Maximin, St-Maximin-la-Ste-Baume

Provence's finest example of Gothic architecture was erected to house the relics of Mary Magdalene, "discovered" on the site in 1280. The basilica appears unfinished from the outside (there is no belfry) but within, the sense of balance is stunning. So too are the treasures, notably a 16th-century altarpiece depicting the Passion and a renowned 17th-century organ. Mary Magdalene's remains are in a reliquary and a marble sarcophagus in the crypt. ☊ *Map D4 • Open 9am–6pm daily (except during Mass) • Free*

Port Grimaud

Troglodyte dwellings, Villecroze

Bormes-les-Mimosas

A glorious village, unravelling down its hillside in a cascade of little streets, stairways and flowers *(see p38)*. ✎ *Map E5*

The Caves, Villecroze

Riddling the wall of rock that dominates the medieval village, these caves were first home to prehistoric folk and, later, provided refuge against marauding Saracens. Most startling, however, is a cave on the north side of the village, transformed by a 16th-century nobleman into a four-storey, fortified house. The Renaissance frontage, staircases and windows cut out of the stone can still be seen. A spring within the caves creates a cascade which waters gardens below. ✎ *Map E4 • Open for guided tours only, Apr: 3–6pm Fri–Mon; May–Jun: 10:30am–12:30pm, 3–6pm Fri–Mon; Jul–Sep: 10am–1pm, 3–7pm daily • Adm*

Musée des Traditions Provençales, Draguignan

Housed in 18th-century buildings in the heart of the old town, this is one of the best ethnographic museums in France. It tells the story of Provençal life from its earliest days to the beginning of the 20th century with tableaux, models, reconstructions and audio-visual devices. ✎ *15 rue Joseph Roumanille • Map F4 • Open 9am–noon, 2–6pm Tue–Sat, 2–6pm Sun • Closed 1 Jan, 1 May, 25 Dec • Adm*

A Day's Drive on the Massif des Maures

Morning

Start in the village of Grimaud and take the D558 up to **La Garde-Freinet** *(see p82)*. Continue 7 km (4 miles) before turning left (D75) towards Gonfaron and stop at the Village des Tortues to see the rare native Hermann tortoise *(Quartier Plaine • Open 9am–7pm daily (to 6pm Dec–Feb) • Adm)*. Take the D39 towards **Collobrières** *(see p82)*. At Col des Fourches head up to Notre-Dame-des-Anges, the Maures's highest point. There's a fascinating chapel and outstanding views.

Three km (2 miles) before Collobrières, turn left (D14) to the Chartreuse de la Verne, a 12th-century Carthusian monastery of local stone *(Quartier Verne • Open 11am–5pm Wed–Mon • Adm)*. Then double back to Collobrières. Stop for a drink or lunch at **La Petite Fontaine** *(see p85)*.

Afternoon

Leave towards Pierrefeu, but 2 km (1 mile) later turn left (D41) towards **Bormes-les-Mimosas**. The dramatic drive, between wooded slopes and plunging valleys, takes you over the Col de Babao to the N98. Turn left towards La Mole, but stop at the Arboretum de Gratte-loup (N98), a forest garden with 50 tree varieties.

Continue to La Mole, then turn right (D27) to the Col du Canadel and stop at the **Domaine du Rayol** gardens *(see p46)*. Returning to Grimaud, reward yourself with dinner at Le Côteau Fleuri *(Pl des Pénitents • 04 94 43 20 17 • Closed Tue • €€)*.

Following pages **Massif de l'Esterel**

Left **Ramatuelle** Right **View from Collobrières**

Var Villages

Le Castellet
The only access to this glorious perched village is via two gates in its 13th-century walls. Within, steep paved streets climb tortuously to the feudal castle. Views over olive groves to the sea are outstanding. ◈ Map D5

Mons
Almost 820 m (2,700 ft) up, Mons has the heritage to match its grandiose position: remains of the great Roche Taillée Roman aqueduct run nearby (see p31). In the village itself, narrow alleys wind around ancient porches, arcades and the wonderful 12th-century church. A gem. ◈ Map F4

Collobrières
It's difficult to resist a village claiming to be "world capital of candied chestnuts". In the heart of the Maures mountains (see p79), Collobrières is surrounded by forested slopes. ◈ Map E5

Les Arcs-sur-Argens
With the medieval castle up top, the rest of the old village hugs the rocky promontory. Its labyrinth of streets and vaulted stairways unfolds to the modern village below. ◈ Map F4

Ramatuelle
Although swamped by the overspill from St-Tropez in summer, Ramatuelle remains a lovely hilltop village. Its tiny streets and vaulted passages are heavy with flowers. ◈ Map F5

La Cadière-d'Azur
The medieval St-Jean gate is a great introduction to this ravishing maze of streets set above the terraced hillsides and vineyards of Bandol. The sun is warm, the air scented and the panorama breathtaking. ◈ Map D5

Tourtour
Remote, perched 600 m (2,000 ft) up and surrounded by pine forest, this is a picturesque tangle of streams, medieval buildings and old stone streets leading to a main square lined with restaurants. ◈ Map F5

Comps-sur-Artuby
This is high, wild country, where the Knights Templar made a base. The 12th-century St-André chapel testifies to their presence, and affords unbeatable views over the nearby Artuby Gorges. ◈ Map F4

La Garde-Freinet
Nestling amid forests of cork-oak and chestnut, La Garde-Freinet stands sentry to the wild Maures Mountains. Higher still are the ruins of the medieval village fortified by Saracens. ◈ Map F5

Callas
Fortified on the side of a green hill, Callas has a winding, self-contained charm imposed by its isolation near the edge of the Canjuers Plateau. It's also a fine base for walking the nearby Pennafort Gorges. ◈ Map F5

Around Provence – The Var & Provençal Coast

Visit the Var villages off-season and you will find a world before tourism took its hold on the region.

Left **Jet-skiing, Var coast** Right **Windsurfers**

🔟 Sporting and Outdoor Activities

1 Watersports
The Var coast offers everything, from sailing and tuna-fishing through to windsurfing and parascending. Resorts awarded the *"Station Voile"* symbol for excellent watersports facilities include Hyères and Bandol. Meanwhile, Brutal Beach at Six-Fours draws international windsurfers *(see p57)* and Cavalaire claims to be the French capital of jet-skiing.

2 Hill Walks in the Maures Mountains
The walking possibilities amid these forests, valleys and peaks are magnificent. Among the best is the two-hour trek from Collobrières to the Chartreuse de la Verne monastery *(see p79)*.

3 Cycling on Porquerolles
Cars are banned, so cycling is the most rewarding way to discover the island. Hire bikes from the village *(see p42)*.

4 Mountain Biking
Tough trail cyclists are spoiled for choice in the Var. The most dramatic trips are around the Verdon gorges *(see pp10–11)* but Draguignan, Figanières and Fréjus also provide challenging routes.

5 Scuba Marine Park, Port-Cros
An underwater guided path. Hire flippers, snorkel and a mask, make for Le Palud beach and follow the buoys to discover posidonia, coral, mother-of-pearl and brightly coloured fish. It is vital you call the tourist office before setting out. ✆ *Tourist office: 04 94 01 40 70*

6 Coastal Walk, St-Tropez
Far from the summer crowds, the path winds around creeks and beaches, vines and pines, offering exceptional views. From Graniers beach to Cap Camarat takes six hours.

7 Golf
The Var has a dozen golf courses, of which the best-known is the Golf de Frégate, set among vineyards and olive groves and overlooking the sea. ✆ *Golf de Frégate, rte de Bandol, St Cyr-sur-Mer • Map E5*

8 Formula One Driving
Try the one-day course, open to all drivers at the Le Luc circuit. Expensive but undeniably thrilling. ✆ *AGS Formule 1, Circuit du Var, Gonfaron • Map F5 • 04 94 60 97 00*

9 Mont Faron
Rising 540 m (2,000 ft) behind Toulon, Mont Faron is most dramatically reached by cable car from blvd Admiral Vence. The views and walks are terrific. ✆ *Map E5*

10 Sailing, Lac Ste-Croix
This vast artificial lake *(see p11)* offers all sorts of boating, from pedalo through to dinghy. It's also an access point for canoe trips up the gorges. ✆ *Map E3*

Left and right **La Playa, Fréjus**

🔟 Var Nightlife

1 Les Caves du Roy, St-Tropez
The Byblos Hotel's legendary club has a suitably strict door policy: the unfashionable are generally unfortunate. Once selected, you're at the heart of Tropezien nightlife *(see p49)*. ⊗ *Ave Paul Signac • Map F5 • www.lescavesduroy.com*

2 Le Papagayo, St-Tropez
This pillar of the resort's jet-set nightlife since 1962 shows no signs of fading. Progress from the terrace restaurant via the cocktail bar to the dance floor, to mingle with the trendy, and famous. ⊗ *Rte Residence du Port • Map F5*

3 Casino des Palmiers, Hyères
Renovated in the 1990s, the casino has retained its *belle époque* style, added on a glass dome and widened its horizons. Alongside the gaming rooms are a hotel, restaurant and nightclub. ⊗ *Ave Ambroise Thomas • Map E6*

4 La Playa, Fréjus
This hotspot livens up the beachfront with outside dance floors. Thursday and Friday evenings offer a buffet dinner then dancing. ⊗ *Fréjus Plage • Map F4*

5 VIP Room, St-Tropez
A Studio 54-like vibe prevails at this exclusive supper/dance club. If you're not eating, don't bother turning up before midnight when the trendy set arrives. ⊗ *Résidence du Nouveau Port • Map F5*

6 Le Saint Hilaire, Sainte-Maxime
Legendary disco with panoramic bay windows facing the sea, and a lounge at the water's edge. Star DJs play a mix of house, electro and R'n'B. ⊗ *27 ave du Général-Leclerc • Map F5*

7 Le Grand Casino, Bandol
A stylish spot in which to play the fruit machines, the tables – or the field – in two different nightclubs: Le Must and Le Blackjack. The complex also boasts a reputable restaurant. ⊗ *Pl Lucien Artaud • Map D5*

8 El Camino de Cuba, Saint-Raphael
Sip a rum-based cocktail while you salsa, mambo and merengue the night away. Dance classes on Mondays, Wednesdays and Sundays. ⊗ *Port Santa-Lucia • Map F5*

9 Le Bora-Bora, Le Lavandou
A brasserie by day, Le Bora-Bora becomes a buzzing music bar by night. Wash down the Latino-Caribbean rhythms with a fine choice of cocktails. ⊗ *Rue Charles Cazin • Map F5*

10 Bar du Port, St-Tropez
This high-tech bar on the port starts early (open for breakfast at 7am) and closes late (4am). The rhythm changes as the day goes by, with lunch and dinner served before DJ-driven house music kicks in. ⊗ *7 quai Suffren • Map F5*

Price Categories	
For a three-course meal for one with half a bottle of wine (or equivalent meal), taxes and extra charges.	€ under €30
	€€ €30–€40
	€€€ €40–€50
	€€€€ €50–€60
	€€€€€ over €60

Above **Hostellerie de l'Abbaye de La Celle**

🔟 Places to Eat

1 Le Bérard, La Cadière d'Azur

This former monastery offers distinctly non-monastic standards of luxury and innovative Provençale cuisine. 🕲 *6 rue Gabriel Péri • Map F5 • 04 94 90 11 43 • Closed Mon, Tue (mid-Jul–mid-Sep: open Tue D) • DA • €€€€€*

2 Le Café, St-Tropez

Fish soup, roast lamb and *tarte tropézienne* are cooked to perfection in this restaurant on St-Tropez's most famous square. 🕲 *Place des Lices • Map F5 • 04 94 97 44 69 • Closed Sun D, Tue • DA • €€€€*

3 Hostellerie de l'Abbaye de La Celle, La Celle

Deceptively simple Provençale fare in lovely 18th-century buildings. 🕲 *10 pl du Général-de-Gaulle • Map F5 • 04 98 05 14 14 • Closed mid-Oct–mid-Apr: Tue & Wed (mid-Jan–early Feb: daily) • DA • €€€€*

4 Café des Jardiniers, Le Rayol-Canadel

Soup, omelette and salads, using fresh produce from these lovely waterside gardens just west of St-Tropez. 🕲 *Le Domaine du Rayol, ave des Belges • Map F5 • 04 98 04 44 05 • Closed Mon & Tue low season • DA • €*

5 Le Logis du Guetteur, Les Arcs-sur-Argens

This 11th-century castle is now a superb restaurant. In winter, dining is in the lookout tower; in summer on the terrace. 🕲 *Pl du Château • Map F4 • 04 94 99 51 10 • Closed mid-Feb–mid-Mar • €€€€€*

6 La Brasserie, St-Raphaël

This hidden gem serves French cuisine on a garden terrace shaded by lemon and magnolia trees. 🕲 *6 ave de Valescune • Map F5 • 04 94 95 25 00 • Closed Sun •€€*

7 L'Ecurie du Castellas, Ramatuelle

Fine Provençal food and stunning views over the Golfe de St-Tropez are on offer here. 🕲 *Rte des Moulins de Paillas • Map F6 • 04 94 79 11 59 • DA • €€€€€*

8 Le Bistrot de Marius, Hyères

Next to a Templar tower in the old town's small square, this is one of the best bistros in the area for fresh regional food. 🕲 *1 pl Massillon • Map E5 • 04 94 35 88 38 • Closed Mon, Tue, mid-Nov–Jan • DA • €€€*

9 La Bastide des Magnans, Vidauban

La Bastide takes the simplest Provençal ingredients and comes up with a balanced array of wonderful tastes. 🕲 *32 ave Maréchal Galliéni • Map F5 • 04 94 99 43 91 • Closed Sun D, Mon • DA • €€€€€*

10 La Petite Fontaine, Collobrières

Excellent, no-frills regional cooking is served in a characterful restaurant on the village square. 🕲 *Pl de la République • Map E5 • 04 94 48 00 12 • Closed Apr–mid-Sep: Sun D, Mon; Oct–Mar: Sun–Mon L, Sun–Thu D; public hols; Feb school holidays; 2 wks Sep • No credit cards • €€*

 Note: *Unless otherwise stated, all restaurants accept credit cards and serve vegetarian meals*

Left **Musée National Marc Chagall** Right **Promenade des Anglais**

Nice

NICE – THE VERY WORD SPARKLES WITH SUNLIGHT AND GLAMOUR. *In the 19th century, the European aristocracy colonized the place, drawn by the glorious curve of the Bay of Angels and the mild winter weather. More recently, it has been the turn of film stars to endow France's fifth city with a legacy of luxury. And there's a legacy of culture, too. Artists such as Matisse and Chagall were inspired by Nice's limpid light and left their mark here with their abstract works (see pp36–7). Alongside this opulence, however, there is another Nice, rooted in Mediterranean history and fiercely independent. The city voted to join France only in 1860 (it had for centuries been part of the kingdom of Savoy) and retains its own Niçois dialect, cuisine and traditions. It is from the marriage of these two different halves that the real fascination of Nice is born.*

Mansion, Cimiez Hill

🔟 Sights

1. **Vieux Nice**
2. **Promenade des Anglais and Promenade du Paillon**
3. **Musée Matisse**
4. **Musée d'Art Moderne et d'Art Contemporain (MAMAC)**
5. **Musée des Beaux-Arts**
6. **Villa Masséna**
7. **Cimiez Hill and Musée National Marc Chagall**
8. **Port Lympia**
9. **Parc Floral Phoenix and Musée des Art Asiatiques**
10. **Cathédrale St-Nicolas**

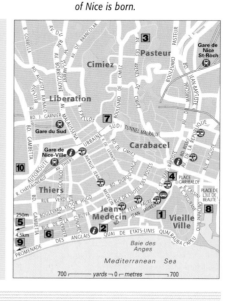

1 Vieux Nice

The city's heart, filled with the aroma and sounds of all things Niçoise (see pp16–17).

2 Promenade des Anglais and Promenade du Paillon

The Promenade des Anglais owes its name to the English community that funded its construction in 1822, to give work to the local poor. Now flanked by traffic lanes, it sweeps majestically round the Bay of Angels, dotted with *Belle époque* edifices, notably the magnificent Hotel Negresco (see p140). In contrast, the Promenade du Paillon cuts a green swathe through the city to the sea. With its central waterway, it provides a tranquil alternative to walking through busy streets, and is also a venue for arts and leisure activities. ❧ Map N4–5

3 Musée Matisse

Shortly before his death in 1954, Matisse (see p36) donated a collection of paintings to the city in which he had lived for 37 years. They have found a superb home in a 17th-century Italianate

Musée d'Art Moderne et d'Art Contemporain

villa on Cimiez Hill. Boosted by subsequent donations, the collection affords a comprehensive overview of the artist's work, from 1890 through to the gouache cut-outs of his later years. It is made all the more effective by the presentation of items from his daily life (see p34). ❧ 164 ave des Arènes de Cimiez • Map Q1 • Open 10am–6pm Wed–Mon • Closed 1 Jan, Easter, 1 May, 25 Dec • Free

4 Musée d'Art Moderne et d'Art Contemporain (MAMAC)

Conceived as a triumphal arch on four marble columns linked by transparent walkways, the museum's modern architecture is startlingly effective. The collections trace the story of the avant garde from the 1960s to the present day. Particularly notable are the US Pop Artists and European New Realists, including Nice's own Yves Klein (see p35). ❧ Place Yves Klein • Map Q4 • Open 10am–6pm Tue–Sun • Closed 1 Jan, Easter, 1 May, 25 Dec • Free

Trompe l'oeil façade, Musée Matisse

5 Musée des Beaux-Arts

The 19th-century townhouse built for a Ukrainian princess is a marvel of Neo-Classical excess. It holds collections of art from the 17th to early 20th centuries. The first floor provides a panorama of 19th-century French art, through to the Impressionists and Post-Impressionists. On the ground floor are 17th- and 18th-century works, including Rodin sculptures. ✪ *33 ave des Baumettes • Map N5 • Open 10am–6pm Tue–Sun • Closed 1 Jan, Easter, 1 May, 25 Dec • Free*

Musée National Marc Chagall

6 Villa Masséna

This elegant, 19th-century Italianate villa houses the Musée d'Art et d'Histoire, which has an interesting collection of diverse objects covering the period from Bonaparte through to the 1930s. Rooms are furnished in First Empire style, and highlights include Napoleon's coronation robe and death mask. ✪ *65 rue de France • Map P5 • Open 10am–6pm Wed–Mon • Closed 1 Jan, Easter, 1 May, 25 Dec • Free*

Nice's Expat Community

Led by the British, European (notably Russian) nobility flocked to Nice in wintertime from the early 19th century. Vast, luxurious hotels, villas and places of entertainment sprung up to accommodate them. Nice became two cities – one for the wealthy and leisured northern visitors and another for working Mediterranean natives. This era disappeared with World War I, but somehow the glamour never left.

7 Cimiez Hill and Musée National Marc Chagall

When European nobility took to wintering in Nice, they colonized Cimiez Hill with magnificent villas in styles from Louis XV, to Neo-Gothic, to Oriental. Most impressive of all is the Excelsior Regina Palace, where Queen Victoria once stayed. Also here is the museum which houses Chagall's 17 great works on the "Biblical Message" (see p36). The collection was supplemented by oils, sketches, pastels and gouaches, donated by the artist. Chagall also created stained-glass windows, a mosaic and tapestry for the museum (see p34). ✪ *Ave du Dr Ménard • Map Q3 • Open 10am–6pm Wed–Mon (to 5pm Nov–Apr) • Closed 1 Jan, 1 May, 25 Dec • Adm*

8 Port Lympia

Dug in the mid-18th century, the port never took off commercially and remains quieter than most Mediterranean city harbours. It is all the more charming for that, a haven of pleasure boats and cruise-ships, surrounded by splendid Italianate buildings. Little wonder that the visiting Russian playwright Chekhov considered this the most pleasing part of Nice. ✪ *Map R4*

9 Parc Floral Phoenix and Musée des Arts Asiatiques

This large floral park is a themed wonderland of world horticulture with, at its centre, Europe's biggest greenhouse. Inside the metal and glass "marquee", one wanders through recreated warm-climate zones, from equatorial forest to the Natal desert. Also in the park is the Asian Arts Museum, a marble and glass construction containing classical and contemporary creations from the main Asian civilizations. ✪ 405 promenade des Anglais • Map N5 • Park: Open 9:30am–6pm daily (to 7:30pm Apr–Sep, to 7pm early Oct, to 6:30pm late Oct); Adm • Museum: Open May–mid-Oct: 10am–6pm Wed–Mon; mid-Oct–Apr: 10am–5pm Wed–Mon; Closed 1 Jan, 1 May, 25 Dec; Free

10 Cathédrale St-Nicolas

The Russian community was almost as prominent in Nice as the British in the late 19th and early 20th centuries. This Russian Orthodox cathedral was completed in 1912 as the community's focal point. ✪ Ave Nicolas II • Map N4 • Open 9am–noon, 2–6pm Tue–Sun • Closed during private religious events • Adm

Cathédrale St-Nicolas

A Morning Walk around Nice

🕐 Start at the Tourist Office (5 promenade des Anglais), then turn left along avenue de Verdun to place Masséna, the city's central square. Take in the glorious red façades, gardens and ornamental fountains before crossing to enter **Vieux Nice** (see pp16–17) on rue Alexander Mari. Turn right into rue de l'Opéra and left into rue St-François-de-Paule, an old-fashioned street with long-established shops, notably Auer for confectionery (No. 7) and Alziari for olive oil (No. 14). Proceed to cours Saleya for the celebrated flower market, then turn into tiny rue Gaëtan to soak up the old town atmosphere. Before leaving the old town, don't fail to take in the cathedral, the magnificent Palais Lascaris, place St-François fish market and the narrow, shop-filled rue Pairolière.

Emerge into the relative peace and 18th-century harmony of place Garibaldi, then take rue Dr-Ciaudo to the splendid **MAMAC** (see p87), where you can spend an hour or so admiring the museum's wonderful modern art. Back in the fresh air, stroll along boulevard Carabacel with its elaborate mansions.

At place Magenta, forget culture and start shopping. For designer fashion proceed into rue Paradis then avenue de Suède. Rue de Rivoli then brings you to the legendary **Hotel Negresco** (see p140). If you're feeling rich, lunch in its **Chantecler** restaurant (see p91); if watching the pennies, have a look anyway: its interior abounds in ornate treasures.

Left **Ma Nolan's** Right **Hotel Negresco, home to Negresco Piano Bar**

Nightspots in Nice

Bar des Oiseaux
Francophiles will enjoy the theme nights – philosophy, sing-songs and cabaret – while the rest can sip a drink amid a lively crowd at this colourful bar in the old town. ✆ Corner of rue St Vincent & rue d'Abbaye • Map Q5 • Closed Sun, Mon pm

La Civette du Cours
"Bar sympa", they say in French, which means friendly and appealing – especially for the young, artistic and mildly eccentric. ✆ 1 cours Saleya • Map Q5

High Club – Studio 47
A popular disco with dance-floors on two levels – the High Club for trendy 20–30-year-olds, and Studio 47 for over-30s preferring a more refined atmosphere. ✆ 45 promenade des Anglais • Map N5

Wayne's
Home-from-home for English people in this pub in Vieux Nice. Good beer, pub food, live music, table dancing and a terrace. ✆ 15 rue de la Préfecture • Map Q5

La Cave Romagnan
One of the oldest wine bars in town, with live music on Saturday nights and local art on the walls. ✆ 22 rue d'Angleterre • Map P4

B Spot
This intimate club offers jazz, funk, blues and more, Thursday to Sunday, and is a venue for the Nice Jazz Festival (see p58). ✆ 24 ave Marechal Foch • Map P4

Negresco Piano Bar
No techno here in the bar of the city's palatial hotel (see p140). Just the tinkling of ivories amid wood panelling and deep armchairs, which give the place the pleasingly languorous air of a gentleman's club. ✆ 37 promenade des Anglais • Map N5

Le Six
In the heart of Vieux Nice, this gay-friendly bar has live music, go-go dancers and karaoke every night in the summer. ✆ 6 rue Raoul Bosio • Map Q5

L'f
Pronounced "Lef", this is a friendly place for a drink and a bite to eat on the Vieux Nice nighttime circuit. A year-round venue – the terrace is heated in winter. ✆ 6 pl Charles Félix • Map P5

Ma Nolan's
The Irish pub to go to in Nice. Pints of Guinness, cooked dinners like grandma used to make, televised sport and free Wi-Fi make this a favourite for expats. (One of two locations.) ✆ 2 rue St-François-de-Paule • Map Q5

Price Categories

For a three-course		€	under €30
meal for one with half		€€	€30–€40
a bottle of wine (or		€€€	€40–€50
equivalent meal), taxes		€€€€	€50–€60
and extra charges.		€€€€€	over €60

Above **La Merenda**

🔟 Places to Eat

1 Le Chantecler
Palatial setting within the Hotel Negresco for Jean-Denis Rieubland's renowned Provençale-inspired *haute cuisine (see p50)*. ⊗ 37 promenade des Anglais • Map N5 • 04 93 16 64 00 • Closed Mon–Tue, Sun L, Jan–mid-Feb • €€€€€

2 Il Vinaino
The fact that this is the local Italians' favourite restaurant says it all. The food is exquisite and the ambience is homely. ⊗ 33 rue de la Buffa • Map P5 • 08 99 23 45 14 • Closed Sun, Mon L • €€

3 La Merenda
Dominique le Stanc turned his back on superchef stress to open this little restaurant. No telephone, no pretension – just simple excellence. ⊗ 4 rue Raoul Bosio • Map P5 • Closed Sat, Sun, bank hols • No credit cards • €€

4 Chez Acchiardo
Locals sip their apéritifs at the counter and from the kitchen comes simple, flavoursome food (fresh fish soup, *tournedos au gorgonzola*). ⊗ 38 rue Droite • Map R5 • 04 93 85 51 16 • Closed Sat, Sun, Aug • No credit cards • No vegetarian dishes • €€

5 Don Camillo
A refined setting on the edge of Vieux Nice for the most refined Niçois cooking available. Try the stuffed ravioli *à la Niçoise*. ⊗ 5 rue des Ponchettes • Map R5 • 04 93 85 67 95 • Closed Sun–Mon, 1–15 Feb • €€€€€

6 Le Boccacio
The decor of this restaurant specializing in seafood recalls that of a schooner – but it's stylish, rather than kitsch. ⊗ 7 rue Masséna • Map R5 • 04 93 87 71 76 • €€

7 Les Viviers
An elegant interior comple-ments classical seafood dishes and impressive desserts. ⊗ 22 rue Alphonse Karr • Map P4 • 04 93 16 00 48 • Closed Sat L, Sun, mid-Jul–Aug • €€€€

8 La Zucca Magica
This vegetarian restaurant at the port serves top-quality Italian dishes and has a good-value daily menu. ⊗ 4 bis quai Papacino • Map R4 • 04 93 56 25 27 • Closed Sun • €€

9 Le Safari
Seafood and meat dishes served on one of the liveliest terraces of Vieux Nice. ⊗ 1 cours Saleya • Map Q5 • 04 93 80 18 44 • €€

10 Nissa Socca
Nissa is Nice, and *socca* is the local chickpea flour pancake, and this is a great place to eat it. ⊗ 7 rue Ste-Réparate • 04 93 80 18 35 • Closed Sun, Jan • No credit cards • €

Note: Unless otherwise stated, all restaurants accept credit cards and serve vegetarian meals

Left **Prince's Palace** Right **Roquebrune-Cap-Martin rooftops**

Monaco and the Riviera

THE FRENCH RIVIERA, *stretching from Cannes to the Italian border, is the most mythologized stretch of Mediterranean coastline. In the 19th century its balmy winter climate attracted plutocrats, princes and their entourages, and its clear sunlight and vivid colours drew a new breed of painters. In the 1920s it became a summer resort for the first time, and in the 1950s and 1960s it was the epitome of jet-set chic and the habitat of film stars, musicians and millionaires. You could say that this is where modern tourism really started. In high summer there seems to be hardly a square metre of beach, a yacht mooring, parking space or café table left vacant, while off-shore or in Antibes' harbour float the cruisers of the mega-rich. This is a coast like no other and all you can do is surrender to its mystique. Meanwhile, the enclave of Monaco, an independent state since the 14th century, has a character all of its own.*

🔟 Sights

1. Casino de Monte Carlo
2. Musée Picasso
3. Prince's Palace
4. Villa Ephrussi de Rothschild
5. Château-Musée Grimaldi
6. Marineland
7. Musée Renoir
8. Roquebrune-Cap-Martin
9. Sales des Mariages
10. Villa Kerylos

Riviera promenade

1 Casino de Monte Carlo

This monument to *belle époque* splendour is also the heart of the region's famous gambling industry – well worth a look whether you want to play the stakes or simply soak up some glamour *(see pp26–7)*.

Picasso ceramic jug, Musée Picasso

2 Musée Picasso, Antibes

A bishop's palace during the Dark Ages, this building then fell into the hands of the Grimaldi lords of Monaco, before becoming the seat of the royal governors of the region. Today, it is one of the finest art galleries in the world. The museum houses 300 works by Spanish artist Pablo Picasso *(see p36)*, who worked here in 1946 and donated drawings, paintings and more than 100 ceramic pieces. Work by other artists, including Léger, Ernst, Modigliani and Miró, is also on display *(see p34)*. ◈ *Château Grimaldi, Vieux Port • Map G4 • Open mid-Jun–mid-Sep: 10am–6pm Tue–Sun (to 8pm Wed & Fri Jul–Aug); mid-Sep–mid-Jun: 10am–noon, 2–6pm Tue–Sun • Closed 1 Jan, 1 May, 1 Nov, 25 Dec • DA • Adm*

3 Prince's Palace, Monaco

Built on the site of a 13th-century Genoese fortress, the seat of the Grimaldi princes of Monaco, flanked by centuries-old cannons, is even more imposing inside than out. Highlights include superb frescoes of mythological scenes by 16th-century Genoese artists, the opulent blue-and-gold Louis XV Salon, the finely crafted woodwork of the Mazarin Salon and the gorgeous Throne Room. The main courtyard, the Cour d'Honneur, with its geometrical pebble patterns, is a wonderful setting for summer concerts. The Compagnie des Carabiniers du Prince, in full dress uniform, changes the guard daily at 11:55am. ◈ *Pl du Palais • Map H4 • Open (State Rooms and Grands Appartements: Apr–Oct: 10am–6pm daily • Adm*

4 Villa Ephrussi de Rothschild, St-Jean-Cap-Ferrat

The most palatial of all the villas built in the Riviera's plutocratic heyday was the dream of Beatrice Ephrussi de Rothschild (1864–1934), a daughter of the wealthy banking family. Its lavish Neo-Classical façade conceals an opulent interior of arcades surrounded by a covered courtyard hung with magnificent tapestries. Superb antiques and sketches by Fragonard also feature, while the gardens are as sumptuous as the interior *(see p46)*. ◈ *1 ave Ephrussi de Rothschild • Map G4 • Open 10am–6pm daily (Nov–Feb: 2–6pm Mon–Fri, 10am–6pm Sat–Sun) • DA to ground floor only • Adm*

Villa Ephrussi de Rothschild

The Grimaldis of Monaco

Monaco's Grimaldi dynasty is the oldest ruling family in the world. François Grimaldi, disguised as a monk, seized the castle in 1297. By 1489 France and Savoy recognized Monaco's independence. In 1612 Honore II was the first lord to take the title of prince. During the French Revolution the prince and his family were ousted, to be restored to their throne in 1814.

5 Château-Musée Grimaldi, Haut-de-Cagnes

Built as a Grimaldi fortress in 1309, this castle's battlements dominate the landscape of Haut-de-Cagnes. Inside the walls, however, is a wonderful surprise: a sumptuous palace, built in 1620 by Jean Henri Grimaldi. Today it houses a clutch of museums and art collections including a museum of modern Mediterranean art, a museum dedicated to the olive tree, and a collection of portraits of the renowned 1930s *chanteuse*, Suzy Solidor. ✪ *9 pl Grimaldi • Map G4 • Open 10am–noon (Jul & Aug: to 1pm), 2–6pm (Nov–Apr: to 5pm) Wed–Mon • Closed 1 Jan, 25 Dec • Adm*

Renoir's studio, Musée Renoir

6 Marineland, Antibes

Killer whales, sharks and dolphins are all inhabitants of Marineland. There is also a farm, a petting zoo, a butterfly and reptile jungle, and the largest water park on the Riviera, with 12 giant chutes, a wave pool, a large swimming pool, as well as 3 miniature golf courses. ✪ *Rte National 7, Antibes • Map G4 • Open hours vary according to season; see www.marineland.fr • DA • Adm*

7 Musée Renoir, Cagnes-sur-Mer

The former home of artist Auguste Renoir has been preserved almost exactly as it was at the time of his death in 1919. Eleven of his paintings are on display, including *Les Grandes Baigneuses* (1892), along with some of his sculptures and works by his friends Raoul Dufy and Pierre Bonnard. ✪ *19 chemin des Collettes • Map G4 • Open Apr–Sep: 10am–noon, 2–6pm Wed–Mon (10am–1pm Jun–Sep); Oct–Mar: 10am–noon, 2–5pm Wed–Mon • Closed 1 Jan, 1 May, 25 Dec • Adm*

Château-Musée Grimaldi courtyard

8 Roquebrune-Cap-Martin

The Château de Roquebrune, perched on its hilltop above Cap-Martin, is said to be the oldest feudal castle in France. Built more than 1,000 years ago, it has been remodelled more than once, by the Grimaldi clan and, in the early 20th century, by a wealthy Englishman, Sir William Ingram. Down at sea level, a lovely coastal path leads all the way to Monaco, passing 19th-century villas set in lush gardens *(see p39)*. ✎ *Map H3 • Château de Roquebrune: pl William Ingram, Open daily; Jun–Sep: 10am–1pm, 2–7pm; Oct–Jan: 10am–12:30pm, 2–5pm; Feb–May: 10am–12:30pm, 2–6pm • Closed public hols, Fri Nov–Jan • Adm*
• www.roquebrune-cap-martin.com

9 Salle des Mariages, Menton

Jean Cocteau decorated this room in Menton's town hall in 1957, adorning it with colourful images of a fishing couple and the tragic story of Orpheus and Eurydice. More of his work can be seen in the Musée Jean Cocteau located on the seafront *(see p34)*. ✎ *Hôtel de Ville, 17 rue de la République • Map H3 • Open 8:30am–noon, 2–4:30pm Mon–Fri • Closed pub hols • Adm*

10 Villa Kerylos, Beaulieu-sur-Mer

Theodore Reinach (1860–1928) created this remarkable building, constructed between 1902 and 1908, as a perfect Classical Greek villa, in imitation of the palace of Delos in Greece, dating from the 2nd century BC. Copies of ancient mosaics and frescoes evoke the world of the Greek city states. ✎ *Impasse Gustave Eiffel • Map F4 • Open mid-Feb–Oct: 10am–6pm daily (Jul & Aug: to 7pm); Nov–mid–Feb: 2–6pm Mon–Fri, 10am–6pm Sat, Sun • DA • Adm • www.villa-kerylos.com*

A Morning Tour of The Rock

🕐 Start this walk around the oldest part of Monaco, where the Grimaldis founded their principality. Visit the state apartments and the **Prince's Palace** *(see p93)*, taking in the lavish salons, throne room and 17th-century chapel. In one wing is the Musée des Souvenirs Napoléoniens *(Open Apr–Nov: 10am–6pm daily; Dec–Mar: 10:30am–5pm daily • Adm)* housing over 1,000 items, including many of Napoleon Bonaparte's personal effects.

From place du Palais it is a short walk along rue Basse, one of the most picturesque streets in the old quarter, to the Museum of the Chapel of the Visitation, on place de la Visitation *(Open 10am–4pm Tue–Sun • Adm)*. Housed in the Baroque chapel are works by artists Rubens and Zurbaran.

At the end of rue Basse, turn right and double back along avenue St-Martin to the Oceanographical Museum *(Open Apr–Sep: 9:30am–7pm Mon–Fri (Jul–Aug to 7:30pm) • Closed Grand Prix Day • Adm)*. You'll need at least 90 minutes here to view the tanks of marine fauna from all over the world. Don't miss the aquarium with its fearsome sharks. Lunch in the museum's restaurant and savour the view of the Riviera and the Esterel hills from its terrace, before rounding off your day with the 30-minute ride on the Azur Express tourist train. This leaves from the museum on a round trip past the port, the palace, casino and ornamental gardens.

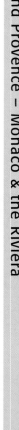

Around Provence – Monaco & the Riviera

➤ *Following pages:* **Monaco harbour**

Left **Plage d'Agay Beach** Right **Port St-Lucia**

Top 10 Beaches and Watersports

Plages de la Croisette
One long beach stretches all the way along the Cannes esplanade, sectioned off into tiny private beaches, with umbrellas, loungers and snack bars with waiter service. Most offer waterskiing. ⊗ Map G4 • Open May–Sep: 8am–sunset daily • Adm

Plage d'Agay
Watersports on this beautiful beach include waterskiing, windsurfing and parascending, as well as more relaxing boat excursions. ⊗ Map G5

Théoule
The pretty beach at Théoule, surrounded by hills, bustles in summer. Kayaks and pedaloes are available for rental. ⊗ Map G4

Port St-Lucia, St-Raphaël
Try eight different watersports including parascending, waterskiing and windsurfing, just outside St-Raphaël, with a one-day discovery pass sold at the tourist office. ⊗ Map F5 • Free • DA

Windsurfers, Côte d'Azur

Vieux Port, St Raphaël
St Raphaël is the coast's top dive centre, with shipwrecks from World War II and a range of wall dives off the rocky coast. There are several dive outfits at the Vieux Port – a list is available from the tourist office. ⊗ Map G5

Yacht Club d'Antibes, Antibes
The club offers windsurfing, dinghy and catamaran sailing and yacht charters for all levels, with crewed yachts available by arrangement. ⊗ Blvd James Wyllie • Map G4 • Open 8am–sunset daily

Plage de la Siesta, Antibes
This beach offers a range of adrenaline sports that includes bungee-jumping, waterskiing and parascending. ⊗ Map G4 • Open Jun–Sep: 9am–sunset daily • Adm • DA

Plage Helios, Juan-les-Pins
Exciting parascending and, for the even more adventurous, breathtaking flights aboard microlight float-planes. ⊗ Map G4 • Open Apr–Sep: 8am–sunset daily • Adm • DA

Marineland
A huge family aquapark with 12 chutes, a wave pool and several swimming pools including one for toddlers (see p94).

Palais des Festivals
Perhaps not the most luxurious beach in Cannes, but it is no more crowded than the pay beaches and it's free. ⊗ Map F4

For the Top 10 best beaches in Provence See pp42–3

Above **Jardin Exotique, Monaco**

ⓘ Riviera Gardens

1 Villa Ephrussi de Rothschild
Gorgeous formal gardens and lily ponds surround the pink-and-white villa built by Beatrice Ephrussi de Rothschild (see p93).

2 Jardin Exotique, Monaco
The largest collection of succulent rock plants in the world, plus a 60-m (200-ft) deep cave with spectacular limestone formations. ✆ 62 blvd du Jardin Exotique • Map H4 • Open daily from 9am. Feb–Apr, Oct: to 6pm; May–Sep: to 7pm; Nov–Jan: to 5pm or dusk • Closed 19 Nov, 25 Dec • Adm • www.jardin-exotique.mc

3 Parc Fontvieille and Princess Grace Rose Garden, Monaco
Palm and olive groves with a lake surround 4,000 roses planted in memory of Princess Grace of Monaco. ✆ Fontvieille • Map H4 • Open sunrise–sunset daily • DA • Free

4 Japanese Garden, Monaco
This formal garden is a triumph of Zen horticulture and a striking contrast to the classic gardens of the Riviera. ✆ Ave Princesse Grace, Monte Carlo • Map H4 • Open 9am–sunset daily • DA • Free

5 Casino Gardens, Monaco
Laid out around the casino (see pp26–7) these are classic 19th-century gardens, with trim lawns and water features. ✆ Pl du Casino, Monte Carlo • Map H4 • Open 9am–sunset daily • Free

6 Jardin Exotique, Eze
The exotic gardens around the clifftop village offer superb sea views. ✆ Rue du Château • Map H4 • Open daily from 9am. Jan: to 4pm; Feb & Mar: to 5pm; Apr, May & Oct: to 6pm; Jun, Sep: to 7pm; Jul & Aug: to 7:30pm; Nov & Dec: to 4:30pm • Adm

7 Jardin Botanique Exotique, Menton
Laid out by Lord Radcliffe in 1905, this garden is planted with sub-tropical shrubs. ✆ Ave St-Jacques • Map H3 • Open Wed–Mon. Apr–Sep: 10am–12:30pm, 2–5pm; Oct–Mar: 10am–12:30pm, 2–5pm • Closed 1 May • Adm

8 Parc Thuret, Cap d'Antibes
Superb collection of trees and shrubs founded by Gustave Thuret in 1857. ✆ 62 blvd du Cap • Map G4 • Open Mon–Fri. Summer: 8am–6pm; winter: 8:30am–5:30pm • Closed pub hols • DA • Free (except groups)

9 Parc de Vaugrenier, Antibes
Many rare plants can be seen in this park, with walking trails and a freshwater lagoon. ✆ Blvd des Groules, RN7 dir Villeneuve Loubet • Map G4 • Open 24 hours daily • DA • Free

10 Villa Eilen Roc Gardens, Cap d'Antibes
Charles Garnier, designer of the Monte Carlo Casino, built this villa in a park with trees from all over the world. ✆ Impasse de Beaumont • Map G4 • Open Oct–Mar: 1–4pm Wed & Sat; Apr–Jun: 10am–5pm Wed & Sat; Jul–Sep: 3–7pm Wed, Sat & Sun • DA • Adm Apr–Sep

For the Top 10 best gardens in Provence **See pp46–7**

Left and right **Designer shops, La Croisette, Cannes**

🔟 Places to Shop

1 La Croisette, Cannes
Cannes' esplanade is a great place for shopping or window-shopping, with famous labels such as Chanel (appropriately, at No. 5), Christian Dior (No. 38), Celine (No. 24), Louis Vuitton (No. 22) and Cartier (No. 57). ✪ *Map G4*

2 Rue d'Antibes, Cannes
For that absolutely fabulous Cannes look, head straight for the Rue d'Antibes and its string of designer boutiques, all breathtakingly expensive and dazzlingly ostentatious. ✪ *Map G4*

3 Avenue des Beaux-Arts and Allée Serge Diaghilev, Monaco
With plenty of cash floating around, Monaco is a magnet for designer shops and *haute couture*. Try these two streets for the latest look. ✪ *Map H4*

4 Vallauris
Vallauris's moribund pottery industry was revived when Picasso took an interest in the craft and more than 100 local potters sell their work on its streets in summer. ✪ *Map G4*

5 Le Marché Forville, Cannes
This open-air market over-flows with flowers, seasonal fruit and vegetables, fresh fish and local products. It's a great place to buy Provençal delicacies to take home. Open daily except Mondays, when it becomes a flea market. ✪ *Map G4*

6 Galerie du Metropole, Monaco
Get the Monaco look at an affordable price at this shopping centre which houses a selection of designer shops selling *prêt-à-porter* clothes, shoes and accessories. ✪ *Map H4*

7 Nouvelles Galeries, Menton
You will find four levels of international designer and brand name clothes and accessories for men, women and children, all under one roof. Free parking, too. ✪ *Rue de la République • Map H4*

8 Cours Masséna, Antibes
One of the last authentic covered markets on the Riviera bustles with life every morning until noon and is perfect for buying all sorts of local deli-cacies to take home. ✪ *Map G4*

9 Antiques Market, Antibes
Rummage through stalls selling everything from cut glass and statuary to antique porcelain, lace, embroidery and linen in search of something small enough to carry home. Thursday and Saturdays, from 8am to noon. ✪ *Rue Aubernon, pl de la Liberté and pl Nationale • Map G4*

10 Villeneuve Loubet
Villeneuve Loubet supports a thriving arts scene and is full of artists' and sculptors' studios where you can invest in an original work of art by a living artist. ✪ *Map G4*

Left **Casino de Monte Carlo** Right **Jimmy'z**

🔟 Riviera Nightspots

1 Casino de Monte Carlo
The epitome of Riviera glamour, luxury and gambling excess *(see pp26–7)*.

2 Le Baoli, Cannes
One of the Riviera's best venues, this cool but expensive club-restaurant attracts the likes of Bono and Naomi Campbell to its Asian-style garden of delights. ⚜ *La Croisette • Map G4 • Open from 8pm Fri–Sat (nightly Apr–Oct and during festivals) • DA • www.lebaoli.com*

3 Le Croisette Casino Barrière, Cannes
Within walking distance of the Palais des Festivals and overlooking the busy Croisette, this casino offers one of the city's largest and most elegant gaming rooms. ⚜ *1 Jetée Albert Édouard/1 Espace Lucien Barrière • Map G4 • Open daily to 3am (to 4am Sat & Sun) • DA • www.lucienbarriere.coml*

4 Carlton Bar, Cannes
Billed as "the place to have a drink in the company of stars", but even during the Film Festival, you are unlikely to rub shoulders with the A list. One of the best bars in Cannes, nonetheless. ⚜ *Carlton InterContinental Cannes, 58 La Croisette • Map G4*

5 Jimmy'z, Monaco
Opened in 1974, Jimmy'z is still *the* place to party in Monaco, attracting the rich, famous and beautiful. Of course all this glamour comes at a steep price.
⚜ *Le Sporting Club, ave Princess Grace • Map H4 • 00 377 98 06 70 68 • Open May–Sep: nightly; Oct–Apr: Wed–Sun*

6 Charly's Bar, Cannes
With its stone-walled, cave-like interior, open-door policy and DJs and dancing every night, the crowds keep coming back to this old favourite. ⚜ *5 rue Suquet • Map G4 • 04 97 06 54 78*

7 Blue Gin, Monaco
As the name suggests gin is the drink of choice here, with 17 different varieties on offer. Most guests, however, come to sit on the terrace and admire the beautiful sea view. ⚜ *The Monte Carlo Bay Hotel, 40 ave Princess Grace • Map H4 • 00 377 98 06 03 60 • DA*

8 Disco 7, Cannes
Loud and louche, Disco 7 (or Le 7 Cabaret) attracts a mixed gay and straight crowd. Techno and transvestism make for a decadent atmosphere. ⚜ *7 rue Rouguière • Map G4*

9 Stars 'N' Bars, Monaco
One of the most popular club-restaurants in Monaco, the trans-atlantic music and menu attracts a young, wealthy clientele. ⚜ *6 quai Antoine 1 • Map H4 • www.starsnbars.com*

10 B.Pub, Cannes
Open every night with DJs or live music, this glitzy club attracts a hip crowd. Don't miss the moment when the bar bursts into flames. ⚜ *22 rue Macé • Map G4*

Left **Chevre d'Or, Eze** Right **Le Cactus, Eze**

🔟 Cafés with Terraces

1 Café de Paris, Monte Carlo
In front of the casino *(see p27)*, under white umbrellas and baskets of flowers with the Mediterranean in the background, the Café de Paris is a delightful place for an *al fresco* meal or a drink. ◈ Pl du Casino • Map H4

2 Majestic Barrière, Cannes
Sip your drinks slowly on this deeply fashionable hotel terrace that attracts the *crème de la crème* of the film business during the International Film Festival. A glass of bubbly here costs as much as a meal in many other spots. ◈ 10 La Croisette • Map G4

3 Carlton Terrace, Cannes
The terrace of the Carlton InterContinental is the top place to see and be seen in Cannes, with a superior view of the bay and promenaders along the Croisette. ◈ Carlton InterContinental Cannes, 58 La Croisette • Map G4

4 La Trattoria, Monte Carlo
Famed chef Alain Ducasse's terrace restaurant serves gourmet antipasti, pizzas and gelati in summer. After dinner, skip the queue to get into Jimmy'z next door *(see p101)* via the private entrance. ◈ Le Sporting d'été, ave Princesse Grace • Map H4 • Open mid-May–mid-Sep

5 Villa Ephrussi de Rothschild, St-Jean-Cap-Ferrat
The villa's delightful tea room and terrace, overlooking beautiful gardens and with panoramic views of the bay of Villefranche, is one of the most pleasant places for a light lunch or tea along the entire Riviera *(see p93)*.

6 Bar du Mas, Mougins
Admire the Grasse countryside as you sip a chilled rosé on the stone terrace of this luxury hotel. A much more affordable option than staying here. ◈ Le Mas Candille, blvd Clément Rebuffel • Map G4

7 Plage de la Garoupe, Cap d'Antibes
Walk along the eastern shore of this exclusive part of the Riviera, and you'll come to a short strip of private beaches with several cafés. ◈ Map G4 • Closed Sun pm

8 Chèvre d'Or, Eze
It's worth staying at this gorgeous chateau hotel just to enjoy breakfast on its clifftop terrace, looking out over the sea below *(see p143)*.

9 Hôtel L'Aiglon, Menton
The seafront at Menton is a solid strip of open-air cafés, but this elegant hotel's café-terrace is the most stylish. ◈ 7 ave de la Madone • Map H3

10 Le Cactus, Eze
If your budget won't stretch to the Chèvre d'Or, this modest café has the same stunning views for a fraction of the price and serves delicious *crêpes*. ◈ 3 rue Brec • Map H4

Price Categories

For a three-course meal for one with half a bottle of wine (or equivalent meal), taxes and extra charges.

€	under €30
€€	€30–€40
€€€	€40–€50
€€€€	€50–€60
€€€€€	over €60

Left **Les Deux Frères, Cap Martin**

10 Places to Eat

1 La Table du Royal, St-Jean-Cap-Ferrat
Le Panorama offers elegant, contemporary cuisine and Riviera views that live up to its name. ⊗ *3 ave Jean Monnet • Map H4 • Closed L Jul–Aug, Dec–mid-Jan • DA • €€€€€*

2 La Cave, Cannes
La Cave has built its reputation since 1989 by consistently serving excellent local food. ⊗ *9 blvd de la République • Map G4 • 04 93 99 79 87 • Closed Mon–Sat L, Sun • €€€*

3 3.14 Resto, Cannes
Purple velvet and chandeliers set the tone in this organic restaurant in a fashionable hotel. ⊗ *Hotel 3.14, 5 rue François-Einesy • Map G4 • 04 92 99 72 09 • Closed Mon • DA • €€€€*

4 La Tonnelle, Île St-Honorat
This restaurant offers splendid views and a fish-based lunch. Wines are made by the resident monks. ⊗ *Map G4 • 04 92 99 18 07 • Closed mid-Nov–mid-Dec • DA • €€€*

5 Les Deux Frères, Roquebrune, Cap Martin
Provençal dishes based on lamb, duck and seafood, are served in this delightful restaurant. ⊗ *Pl des Deux Frères • Map H4 • 04 93 28 99 00 • Closed Sun D, Mon, Tue L • €€€€€*

6 L'Auberge Provençale, Antibes
Traditional Provençal dishes are served in a flower-filled courtyard. ⊗ *61 pl Nationale • Map G4 • 04 93 34 13 24 • Closed Sun D, Mon • DA • €€€€€*

7 Bacon, Cap d'Antibes
This legendary fish restaurant has spectacular views over the Baie des Anges. ⊗ *668 blvd de Bacon • Map G4 • 04 93 61 50 02 • Closed Mon L, Tue L, Nov–Feb • DA • €€€€€*

8 L'Auberge Fleurie, Villeneuve Loubet
Eat Peach Melba just steps from the birthplace of the dish's creator, Escoffier. ⊗ *Rue des Mesures • Map G4 • 04 93 73 90 92 • Closed Mon & Tue L, Wed (summer), Sun D (winter), last wk Mar, 1st wk Jun, 2nd wk Nov • DA • €€€€*

9 Pulcinella, Monte Carlo
Delicious Italian food is the speciality in this lovely restaurant. Photos of celebrity regulars line the walls. ⊗ *17 rue du Portier • Map H4 • 00 377 93 30 73 61 • DA • €€€€*

10 Josy-Jo, Haut-de-Cagnes
Ivy-covered restaurant in a pretty village, serving grilled meat Provençale style. ⊗ *8 rue de Planastel • Map G4 • 04 93 20 68 76 • Closed Sun, Mon • No veg options • €€€€*

Josy-Jo, Haut-de-Cagnes

Note: Unless otherwise stated, all restaurants accept credit cards and serve vegetarian meals

Left **Mosaic, Musée Fernand Léger, Biot** Right **Grasse**

Alpes-Maritimes

TECHNICALLY, THE RIVIERA IS PART OF *the Alpes-Maritimes département,*
but inland from the coastal highway the landscape changes dramatically
and the region's forested mountains, deep river gorges and medieval hilltop
villages seem a million miles from the busy seaside resorts. High in the
mountains is the Parc National du Mercantour, a region of rocky summits
and glaciers which shelters chamois, ibex and rare lammergeier vultures.
In winter heavy snowfall makes this one of France's favourite ski areas.

🔟 Sights

1. Vence
2. Vallée des Merveilles & Musée des Merveilles
3. Fondation Maeght, St-Paul-de-Vence
4. Biot
5. Gorges du Cians
6. Forêt de Turini
7. Gorges du Loup
8. Grasse
9. Vallée de la Vesubie
10. La Trophée des Alpes

Alpes-Maritimes landscape

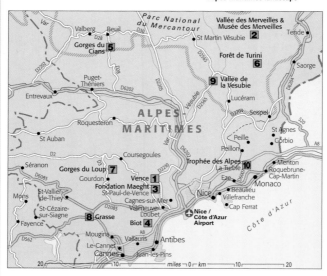

Vence
A gem of the region, with an unbeatable location on a high crag and sweeping views. The old medieval centre is ringed by formidable battlement walls and is entered through a massive stone gateway, to a labyrinth of cobbled streets and tall stone houses. A small cathedral, dating from the 11th century, stands on place Clemenceau. ✎ Map G4

Chagall painting, Fondation Maeght

Vallée des Merveilles and Musée des Merveilles
High in the Parc National de Mercantour (see p40), this valley shelters a treasury of Bronze Age art (see p60). Rock carvings dating from 1800–1500 BC are scattered over the slopes of the 2,870-m (9,400-ft) Mont Bégo. They are almost impossible to find without a guide, but there are fascinating examples in the Musée des Merveilles. ✎ Map H2 • Musée des Merveilles: ave du 16 Septembre 1947, Tende; Open 10am–6:30pm Wed–Mon (to 5pm mid-Oct–Apr; daily Jul–Sep); Closed 1 Jan, 2 wks mid-Mar, 1 May, 2 wks mid-Nov, 25 Dec; Free; DA

Fondation Maeght, St-Paul-de-Vence
One of the finest small modern art museums in the world, the Maeght Foundation includes work by Marc Chagall, Joan Miró, Fernand Léger, Alberto Giacometti, Alexander Calder and many more 20th-century artists. The collection is exhibited in rotation, and the only works on permanent display are the large sculptures in the lovely grounds (see p34). ✎ Montée des Trious • Map G4 • Open 10am–6pm daily (Jul–Sep: to 7pm) • Adm

Biot
The pretty little town of Biot sits serenely on a hilltop among pinewoods. It is renowned for its high-quality decorative glassware, which you can watch being blown at La Verrerie de Biot. The modern Musée Fernand Léger contains more than 400 drawings and paintings by the artist (see p34). ✎ Map G4 • Musée Fernand Léger: Chemin du Val-de-Pome; Open 10am–5pm Wed–Mon (to 6pm May–Oct); Closed 1 Jan, 1 May, 25 Dec; Adm; www.musee-fernandleger.fr • La Verrerie de Biot: Chemin des Combes; Open 9:30am–8pm Mon–Sat (to 6pm in winter), 10:30am–1:30pm, 2:30–7:30pm Sun & pub hols (to 6:30pm in winter); Adm; www.verreriebiot.com • www.biot.fr

Fondation Maeght

Vallée de la Vesubie

semi-tropical luxuriance and huge pines rise on the higher mountainsides. From Pointe des Trois Communes, on the fringe of the forest at an altitude of 2,082 m (6,830 ft), there is a quite breathtaking panorama of the Alpine foothills and the Parc National de Mercantour *(see p40)*. ✦ *Map H3*

Gorges du Cians

The deep gorge carved through the mountains by the River Cians is made all the more spectacular by the deep red of the exposed rock. The river descends 1,600 m (5,250 ft) in just 25 km (15 miles) between the eyrie village of Beuil and Touet-sur-Var, where the Cians meets the larger river Var. The canyon is at its narrowest and most spectacular at Pra d'Astier, around midway between the two villages *(see p41)*. ✦ *Map G3*

Forêt de Turini

A moist micro-climate, created by warm sea air rising over the cooler mountains, waters this mountain forest, where thick beech, maple and chestnut woods cloak the lower slopes in

---

Skiing in the Alpes d'Azur

High above the balmy coast, the summits and slopes of the Alpes d'Azur are deeply covered in snow in winter, with excellent skiing conditions, and there are more than 250 pistes, ranging from black to green runs, in well-equipped resorts. The best known is Isola 2000, with 5 black runs, 14 red, 13 blue and 4 green, suitable for skiers of all levels.

Gorges du Loup

The most spectacular of the region's river canyons. Here the River Loup has sliced its way deep into the limestone rock to create a series of waterfalls including the 40-m (130-ft) Cascade de Courmes, churning rapids and deep potholes such as the Saut du Loup *(see p41)*. ✦ *Map G3*

Grasse

Grasse is a rather unprepossessing town at first sight, but the air is scented by the perfume factories for which it has been famous for more than four centuries. Vast quantities of blossoms are processed here for their essential oils, and a jasmine festival is held each year in August. You can buy perfumes in the shop of the Musée Internationale de la Parfumerie *(see p54)*. ✦ *Map G4 • Musée Internationale de la Parfumerie: 2 blvd du Jeu du Ballon; Open May–Sep: 10am–7pm daily; Oct–Apr: 11am–6pm Wed–Mon (Apr: daily); Closed 1 Jan, 1 May, 25 Dec; Adm*

Vallée de la Vésubie

Two streams merge at St-Martin-Vésubie to form the River Vesubie, which flows through landscapes of pinewoods, flower meadows, forested peaks and narrow canyons to join the Var

Grasse

24 km (15 miles) north of Nice. The valley is dotted with attractive villages, and the river is at its most scenic where it passes through the Gorges de la Vesubie, a canyon of coloured rock walls.
⊘ Map H3 • www.vesubian.com

La Trophée des Alpes
Also known as the Trophée d'Auguste, this remarkable Roman monument is the only building of its kind still in existence. Its towering columns can be seen from afar and there are views along the Riviera. A museum shows a video about the monument's history (see p30).
⊘ Cours Albert 1er, La Turbie • Open Tue–Sun. Mid-Sep–mid-May: 10am–1:30pm, 2:30–5pm; mid-May–mid-Sep: 9:30am–1pm, 2:30–6:30pm • Closed public hols • Adm

La Trophée des Alpes

A Walk through Medieval Vence

🕐 A giant ash tree, Le Frêne (The Ash) is your landmark for the beginning of this two-hour stroll through the old quarter of **Vence** (see p105), with its stone-paved streets and medieval houses huddling inside a ring of 13th-century battlements. Before entering the walls through the 16th-century Porte de Peyra, visit the Château de Villeneuve, which hosts a changing programme of contemporary art and design exhibitions.

After walking through the gateway, turn right, and allow half an hour to walk along the rue du Marché,
🅞 where the rows of shops selling herbs, fruit, fresh pasta and fish will make your mouth water. At the end of the rue du Marché, turn left and walk across place Surian and place Clemenceau to the cathedral – look out for Roman inscriptions dating back almost 2,000 years on the masonry of the buildings either side of it, carved when Vence was the Roman settlement of Vintium. Also look for the oak choir stalls carved with little satirical figures, commissioned by a witty 17th-century bishop.

Leave the square by its north side, through the arched Passage Cahors, then walk up rue du Seminaire and turn left to follow the old walls along rue de la Coste. Leave the old quarter by the Portail Levis, which takes you back on to place du Frêne.
🅞 There are several cafés and restaurants here, such as **Auberge des Seigneurs** (see p109) where you can enjoy a drink and snack.

Left **Gourdon** Right **Peillon**

🔟 Mountain Villages

St-Paul-de-Vence
The prettiest and best known of the region's *villages perchés* (*see p78*), St-Paul was first built as a refuge from Saracen raiders. From its ramparts there are terrific views down to the sea (*see p38*). ✎ *Map G4*

Puget-Théniers
The village stands where the Roudoule river meets the Var, overlooked by the ruins of the Château-Musée Grimaldi (*see p94*). The Romanesque church has a beautiful 16th-century altarpiece (*see p33*). ✎ *Map G3*

St-Cézaire
This hill village has been settled since the Roman era and has medieval walls and watch towers. Nearby are the grottoes of St-Cézaire, an underground wonderland. ✎ *Map G3 • Grottes de St-Cézaire: rte de Grasse; Open 10:30am–6:30pm daily (Sep–May: 10:30am–noon, 2–5:30pm); Closed mid-Nov–Jan; Adm*

Gourdon
From the village square, where the hillside drops into a limestone gorge, you can see all the way down the Loup valley to the coast. ✎ *Map G3*

Peillon
Peillon's red-tiled houses seem to grow out of the hilltop itself,

rising in tiers to a cobbled square with great views of the forested valley. It seems barely changed since the Middle Ages. ✎ *Map H3*

Sospel
Colourful arcaded houses and a Baroque church are features of this pretty mountain village near the Italian border. Badly damaged in World War II, it has been lovingly restored. ✎ *Map H3*

Luceram
Here, tall old houses are set around a 17th-century rococo church and an onion-domed clock tower. ✎ *Map H3*

Saorge
The clifftop location rivals Gourdon's for dizzying effect, and the village is a little changed crescent of 15th–17th-century pastel houses. It has two pretty churches, and magnificent views. ✎ *Map H3*

La Brigue
Unspoilt La Brigue has cobbled streets, arcaded buildings and the Notre-Dame-des-Fontaines with its superb medieval frescoes. ✎ *Map G2*

St-Agnès
At 671 m (2,200 ft) St-Agnès is the highest of the coastal *villages perchés*. There is fine walking nearby, in the Gorbio valley. ✎ *Map H3*

Statue, Puget-Théniers

For Provence's Top 10 villages **See pp38–9**

Price Categories

For a three-course meal for one with half a bottle of wine (or equivalent meal), taxes and extra charges.	€ under €30
	€€ €30–€40
	€€€ €40–€50
	€€€€ €50–€60
	€€€€€ over €60

Left **Auberge de la Madone, Peillon**

🔟 Places to Eat

1 Les Terraillers, Biot

This sophisticated restaurant is set in a 16th-century pottery mill. The dishes are rich and flavourful and the wine list superb. ⊗ *11 rte Chemin Neuf • Map G4 • 04 93 65 01 59 • Closed Wed, Thu, mid-Oct–Nov • €€€€€*

2 Bastide St-Antoine, Grasse

This restaurant serves gastronomic dishes such as scallops with krystal caviar on palm-tree shoots flavoured with lime juice. ⊗ *48 ave Henri Dunant • Map G4 • 04 93 70 94 94 • DA • €€€€€*

3 Le St-Paul, St-Paul-de-Vence

Part of a stunning hideaway hotel, Le St-Paul serves free seafood and other dishes on a terrace with views from the village battlements, or in a stylish dining room. ⊗ *86 rue Grande • Map G4 • 04 93 32 65 25 • Closed Tue–Wed in winter • €€€€€*

4 Le Jarrier, Biot

Hidden away in a side street, this restaurant offers value for money, a pretty terrace and live music at weekends. ⊗ *30 passage de la Bourgade • Map G4 • 04 93 95 93 21 • Closed Mon, Tue • €€*

5 Auberge des Seigneurs, Vence

Renowned spit-roasted local lamb and chickens are among the mouth-watering choices at this friendly medieval inn on the edge of the old quarter, complete with open fire. ⊗ *Pl du Frêne • Map G4 • 04 93 58 04 24 • Closed Sun, Mon, Nov–Feb • No vegetarian options • DA • €€*

6 Auberge de la Madone, Peillon

Enjoy classic Provençal cuisine on a terrace overlooking a medieval village. ⊗ *3 pl Auguste Arnulf • Map H3 • 04 93 07 91 17 • Closed Wed, mid-Nov–Jan • €€€€€*

7 Les Bacchanales, Vence

Chef Christophe Dufau uses simple, local ingredients to create inventive, masterful modern European cuisine. ⊗ *247 ave de Provence • Map G4 • 04 93 24 19 19 • Closed Tue, Wed, 1 week Jun, Dec • DA • €€€€€*

8 Les Templiers, Vence

Another gourmet choice, with some truly excellent dishes such as tagliatelle with cepes and truffles. ⊗ *39 ave Joffre • Map G4 • 04 93 58 06 05 • Closed Mon • €€€€€*

9 La Farigoule, Vence

Unpretentious restaurant with an array of seafood, meat and vegetarian dishes. ⊗ *15 ave Henri-Isnard • Map G4 • 04 93 58 01 27 • Closed Tue–Wed, Sun D, Jan, Dec • €€*

10 Hostellerie Jerome, La Turbie

Inventive dishes such as scampi in a verveine crust. Dinner only. ⊗ *20 rue Comte de Cessole • Map H3 • 04 92 41 51 51 • Closed Mon–Tue (except Jul & Sep), Nov–mid-Feb • €€€€€*

Note: *Unless otherwise stated, all restaurants accept credit cards and serve vegetarian meals*

Left **Rocky landscape outside Sisteron** Right **Lavender fields, Valensole**

Alpes-de-Haute-Provence

ONE OF THE HIGHEST AND WILDEST PARTS OF FRANCE, *and indeed Europe, Alpes-de-Haute-Provence presents a sharp contrast to the foothills and valleys of the Var to the south and the rolling Vaucluse to the west. Summers are hot, winters are bitterly cold and life in these harsh mountains is hard – which is why so much of Haute-Provence is sparsely inhabited. The Durance river flows through the region to meet the Rhône north of Aix, and tributaries such as the Verdon cut spectacular gorges through the limestone rock of the mountains, adding to the breathtaking views, cool clear air and pocket wildernesses of this beautiful region. The area also offers a range of sports from white-water canoeing, to hang-gliding, to high-country walking.*

🔟 Sights

1. Parc Naturel Régional du Verdon
2. Citadelle de Sisteron
3. Mont Pelat
4. Fort de Savoie, Colmars
5. Lurs
6. Ville Forte, Entrevaux
7. Moustiers-Sainte-Marie
8. Musée de la Préhistoire des Gorges du Verdon
9. Montagne de Lure
10. Forcalquier

Moustiers-Sainte-Marie

1 Parc Naturel Régional du Verdon

Along the river Verdon, this regional park is a huge patchwork of landscapes from the neatly cultivated lavender fields of the sunlit Valensole plateau *(see p55)* to the forested hills and pastures of the Artuby, the awesome chasms of the Grand Canyon du Verdon *(see pp10–11)* and the beginnings of the Alps. There are brilliant blue lakes created where the Verdon has been dammed. This is a paradise for hikers, with a network of 700 km (450 miles) of paths, bridleways and ancient mule highways. ✎ *Map E3*

2 Citadelle de Sisteron

Squatting on a steep-sided crag, high above the narrow valley of the River Durance, the formidable defences of the Citadelle guard one of the strategic gateways to Provence *(see p39)*. Built in the 13th century, the bastions and ramparts, crowned by towers and a graceful chapel, are an awesome piece of military engineering. In summer, they become the venue for the Nuits de la Citadelle, a festival of music, theatre and dance. ✎ *Pl de la Citadelle • Map E2 • Open Apr–Nov: from 9am daily (Apr & Oct: to 6pm; May: to 6:30pm; Jun & Sep: to 7pm; Jul & Aug: to 7:30pm; Nov: to 5pm); other times by appt only (call 04 92 61 27 57) • Adm*

Citadelle de Sisteron

3 Mont Pelat

The highest peak in the Provençal Alps rises to a height of 3,050 m (10,020 ft) and dominates a lofty landscape of bare rocky summits, streaked by snow until early summer, pine forests and alpine meadows. The massif is crossed by breath-taking passes, including the Cime de la Bonette, by which the D64 road traverses the shoulder of Mont Pelat at a height of 2,860 m (9,400 ft), making it the highest pass in Europe. ✎ *Map F2*

4 Fort de Savoie, Colmars

Perched atop medieval walls, this 17th-century fortress has a grim, businesslike look when compared with the fairytale medieval castles found else-where in Provence. It was built to withstand cannon fire, not just arrows and siege towers. The

Fort de Savoie, Colmars

work of master military engineer Vauban, it is a testimony to his skill. The Fort de France, the second of this former frontier garrison's strongholds, has fared less well and lies in ruins. 🔍 *Map F2 • Open Jul–Aug: 10am daily for guided tours; Sep–Jun: by appt • Adm*

Lurs

Founded before the reign of Charlemagne, during the Dark Ages, the town of Lurs was fortified as early as the 9th century AD, when it was ruled by the bishops of Sisteron and the princes of Lurs. Deserted in the 19th century, it has now become an artists' colony. There are stupendous views from the Promenade des Evêques (Bishops' Walk) leading to the chapel of Notre-Dame-de-Vie, especially colourful in spring when the wildflowers bloom. 🔍 *Map D2*

Ville Forte, Entrevaux

The citadel of Entrevaux is one of the most dramatic of all the region's many fortresses. Perched on a pinnacle above the fairytale town, it can be reached only by a zig-zag path which passes through more than a dozen arched gateways. Lying beneath it, the impregnable Ville Forte is ringed by towers and ramparts and reached by a drawbridge. 🔍 *Map F3*

Napoleon at Sisteron

On 1 March 1815 Napoleon Bonaparte escaped from exile on Elba and landed at Golfe Juan. Had the citadel at Sisteron been garrisoned by Royalist troops, his attempt to regain his Imperial throne might have been foiled, but he entered the town unopposed on 5 March to begin a triumphal progress to Paris, only to meet final defeat at Waterloo.

Entrevaux citadel

Moustiers-Sainte-Marie

Moustiers, loud with the sound of a swift-running stream which flows through the middle of the village, is simply delightful, with its tall old houses, shady plane trees and, for those who can face the climb, a superb view of the Gorges du Verdon from the clifftop church of Notre-Dame-de-Beauvoir *(see p38)*. The village was and is famed for its faïence ware, and you can see wonderful examples in the Musée de la Faïence *(see p38)*. 🔍 *Map E3 • Musée de la Faïence: rue Bourgade; Open Apr–Oct: 10am–12:30pm, 2–6pm Wed–Mon (to 7pm daily Jul, Aug); Nov–Mar: 2–5pm Sat, Sun & school hols; Closed Jan; Adm (free Tue)*

Musée de la Préhistoire des Gorges du Verdon

This museum, in a building designed by British architect Norman Foster, traces the geological, cultural and environmental evolution of human life in the Verdon and throughout Europe, with an imaginative and fascinating series of displays and interactive exhibits. Guided visits to the caves, where relics of early humans have been discovered, are offered. ⊗ *Rte de Montmeyan, 04500 Quinson • Map E3 • 04 92 74 09 59 for cave tours • Museum open Feb–Mar & Oct–mid-Dec: 10am–6pm Wed–Mon (to 7pm Apr–Jun, Sep); Jul, Aug: 10am–8pm daily • Closed mid-Dec–Jan • Adm*

9 Montagne de Lure

Deep in the heart of the Luberon, the Lure mountain – an extension of the savage massif of Mont Ventoux in neighbouring Vaucluse *(see p117)* – is Provence at its wildest, least hospitable and, some would say, its loveliest. Abandoned hamlets are reminders of Provence in the first half of the 20th century, when many rural people gave up trying to scrape a living from this harsh countryside. ⊗ *Map D2*

Notre-Dame-du-Borguet in Forcalquier

10 Forcalquier

This beguiling old town was once the seat of powerful local lords and capital of the region. One gate of the old walled town, the Porte des Cordeliers, still survives, along with the restored cloisters and stark library of the 13th-century Couvent des Corde-liers, with its tombs of the town's medieval *seigneurs*. The convent is now the seat of the European University of Scents and Flavours. ⊗ *Map D3 • Couvent des Cordeliers: blvd des Martyrs. Contact the Tourist Office to arrange a visit (04 92 75 10 02) • www.forcalquier.com*

A Morning Drive through the Canyon

🕐 Start after breakfast from the unassuming town of **Castellane** *(see p114)*, gateway to the canyons, and drive west on RD952. The landscape becomes progressively more awe-inspiring as you enter the gorges and wind your way through towering walls of rock to **Point Sublime** *(see p11)*. This is one of the most impressive viewpoints; savour it while enjoying a coffee or a cold drink at the pleasant **Auberge du Point Sublime** *(see p115)*.

From here, drive for about 15 minutes and turn left on to the vertiginous Route des Crêtes, which winds past a series of ever higher viewpoints. Don't rush this part of the drive, but stop at each for five or ten minutes, as the views vary all the time. Finally, the road swings around the shoulder of the massif, and far below you is the Verdon and the plateau country around the little village of **La-Palud-sur-Verdon** *(see p114)*. It will take you another 30 minutes to get there, so relax when you do with another coffee at one of the village restaurants.

From La-Palud it's a less daunting drive until the gorgeous turquoise waters of the **Lac de Ste-Croix** *(see p11)* come into sight. The road runs high above the lake, bringing you to the delightfully pretty village of **Moustiers-Ste-Marie**. Reward yourself with lunch here: the village has two of the region's best restaurants, **La Treille Muscate** and **Les Santons** *(see p115)*.

Left **Seyne-les-Alpes countryside** Right **Bar, Castellane**

TOP 10 Towns and Villages

1 Les Mées
Tucked away in the hills, the little village of Les Mées is best known for the strange rock formations known as the Pénitents des Mées. Legend says these pinnacles were once monks who broke their vows of chastity and were turned to stone by St Donat *(see p60)*. ✎ *Map E3*

2 Simiane-la-Rotonde
The enigmatic Rotonde, a Roman relic whose purpose is still a puzzle, crowns the village to which it lends its name, a picturesque cluster of old houses and churches protected by a ramshackle medieval fort. ✎ *Map E3*

3 Seyne-les-Alpes
Military and religious architecture are scattered throughout this quiet mountain town: a 15th-century gate, a medieval church and a ruined citadel are the main points of interest. ✎ *Map E2*

4 Annot
Annot stands in unspoilt countryside in the Vaire valley. Many houses are built into the giant sandstone glacial boulders, known as the *grès d'Annot* – some have 17th- and 18th-century carved façades. ✎ *Map F3*

5 La-Palud-sur-Verdon
La-Palud stands on the north side of the Grand Canyon du Verdon, making it a popular base for exploring the region *(see pp10–11)*. ✎ *Map E3*

6 Castellane
Castellane is a lively market town surrounded by steep mountains. The Verdon flows through it on its way to the Grand Canyon. It is also a centre for adventure sports *(see p11)*. ✎ *Map E3*

7 Allemagne en Provence
Allemagne en Provence stands between the rugged canyon country of the Verdon and the lavender fields of the Valensole plateau. It is dominated by the splendidly palatial Château d'Allemagne, founded in the 12th century. ✎ *Map E3*

8 St-André-les-Alpes
This little village bustles in summer. Built where the Verdon and Issole rivers flow into the manmade Lac de Castillon, it is a popular watersports centre, with dinghies, windsurfers and canoes for hire. ✎ *Map F3*

9 Beauvezer
Beauvezer, in the dramatic Vallée du Haut Verdon, stands 1,179 m (3,600 ft) above sea level. Once a frontier fortress, it still has its formidable battlements. ✎ *Map E3*

10 Barcelonnette
Provence's northernmost town stands in the rugged Ubaye valley, high in the Alps. Its architecture and festivals may have a Mexican influence but its rooftops sometimes see a dusting of snow as late as June. ✎ *Map F1*

Price Categories

For a three-course meal for one with half a bottle of wine (or equivalent meal), taxes and extra charges.		
	€	under €30
	€€	€30–€40
	€€€	€40–€50
	€€€€	€50–€60
	€€€€€	over €60

Above **La Treille Muscate, Moustiers-Ste-Marie**

TOP 10 Places to Eat

1 Le Grand Paris, Digne

The restaurant of Digne's best hotel serves classic dishes with a modern twist. *Hôtel du Grand Paris, 19 blvd Thiers • Map E2 • 04 92 31 11 15 • Closed Mon L, Tue L, Wed L in winter • DA • €€€€€*

2 La Pie Margot, Dauphin

It really is worth travelling 6 km (4 miles) southeast out of Forcalquier to taste the classic cuisine of this small, welcoming restaurant, with views over the valley. *rue du Barri • Map D3 • 04 92 79 51 94 • Closed mid-Dec–Jan • €€*

3 La Treille Muscate, Moustiers-Ste-Marie

Excellent food such as *pistou* of summer vegetables is served in this lovely hotel, with a terrace overlooking the stream. *Pl de l'Eglise • Map E3 • 04 92 74 64 31 • Closed: Jan, Mar–mid-Nov, Dec: Wed D, Thu; mid–end Nov, Feb: Wed, Thu; Jul, Aug: Wed • €€€*

4 Les Santons, Moustiers-Ste-Marie

Close to La Treille Muscate is this pretty restaurant with a leafy terrace. *Pl Pomey • Map E3 • 04 92 74 66 48 • Closed Mon D, Tue • €€€€*

5 Hostellerie de la Fuste, Valensole

Award-winning meals produced from home-grown produce, fresh fish and local lamb, in the heart of the lavender fields. *La Fuste • Map E3 • 04 92 72 05 95 • Closed Sun D, Mon • DA • €€€€€*

6 Le Petit Lauragais, Manosque

The cuisine of southwest France reigns in this intimate restaurant located in the market square. *6 pl du Terreau • Map D3 • 04 92 72 13 00 • Closed Wed L, Sat L, Sun, 1 wk in Mar, mid-Jul–mid-Aug • €€*

7 La Table de Pauline at Villa Borghese, Gréoux-les-Bains

The award-winning chef changes the menu daily. The Provençal dishes are prepared with local, seasonal ingredients. Great choice of fish. *Ave des Thermes • Map E3 • 04 92 78 00 91 • DA • €€€*

8 Auberge du Point Sublime, Rougon

The location makes this inn special, with a terrace gazing out at the peaks of the Canyon du Verdon. The food is reasonable. *Point Sublime • Map E3 • 04 92 83 69 15 • Closed Thu, mid-Oct–Easter • €*

9 L'Olivier, Dignes-les-Bains

This great little restaurant with a terrace offers great value for money. Traditional French cooking with a touch of originality. *1 rue des Monges • Map E2 • 04 92 31 47 41 • Closed Mon, Tue • €€*

10 Au Romarin, Sisteron

Enjoy dishes using regional produce, such as the house speciality courgette (zucchini) gratin, in this cosy, vaulted dining room. Great value menus. *103 rue Saunerie • Map E2 • 04 92 34 88 04 • €€*

***Note:** Unless otherwise stated, all restaurants accept credit cards and serve vegetarian meals*

Left **Pont St-Bénézet, Avignon** Right **Roman theatre, Orange**

Vaucluse

AT THE NORTHERN GATES OF PROVENCE, *the Vaucluse exudes a cultured air. Its rich past – Roman inheritance in Orange, papal legacy in Avignon – is amplified by summer festivals in both towns, while the perched villages of the Luberon seem purpose-built for holiday homes. But the villages are not perched by accident and Avignon's ramparts were not for show – defence was the motive for both. On Mont Ventoux, the Monts de Vaucluse or remote parts of the Luberon, you're in Provence at its most elemental.*

Sights

1. Vaison-la-Romaine
2. Abbaye Notre-Dame de Sénanque
3. Mont Ventoux
4. Roman Theatre, Orange
5. Parc Naturel Régional du Luberon
6. Gorges de la Nesque
7. Fontaine-de-Vaucluse
8. Les Dentelles de Montmirail
9. Synagogue, Carpentras
10. Cathédrale St-Anne, Apt

Avignon

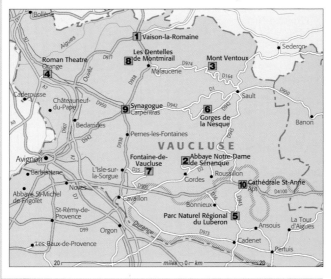

Vaison-la-Romaine
One of the best preserved Roman towns in Provence *(see pp22–3)*.

Abbaye Notre-Dame de Sénanque
When the summer lavender flowers, this medieval abbey surrounded by purple fields is a spectacular sight *(see pp24–5)*.

Mont Ventoux
The bald-headed "Giant of Provence" is the Vaucluse's greatest landmark, a vast pyramid of rock which has inspired poets, mystics and botanists for centuries. Rising 1,900 m (6,300 ft), it commands the surrounding landscape, affording astonishing views to the sea, the Alps and the Rhône. Snow-capped in winter, the summit is revealed as arid chalk in summer and buffeted by strong winds all year round. The lower slopes are dense with trees, 1,000 plant varieties and wildlife. ◈ *Map C2*

Roman Theatre, Orange
The finest Roman theatre in Europe has its original stage wall, guaranteeing perfect acoustics *(see p30)*.
◈ *Rue Madeline Roch • Map B2 • Open daily. Apr–Sep: 9am–6pm (to 7pm Jun–Aug); Oct–Mar: 9:30am–4:30pm (to 5:30pm Mar, Oct) • Adm*

Parc Naturel Régional du Luberon
The Luberon has a wild, mountain beauty and it is the park's job to maintain the balance between tourists and the environment.

Vaison-la-Romaine

Covering 1,500 sq km (600 sq miles), it takes in the rugged Petit Luberon of crags, gorges and perched villages to the west and the more rounded Grand Luberon to the east. It also stretches north to the Monts de Vaucluse. The park's headquarters in Apt have information on walks, the ecology and the area's traditions *(see p40)*.
◈ *Maison du Parc, 60 pl Jean-Jaurès • Map C3 • Open 8:30am–noon, 1:30–6pm Mon–Fri (also Sat am, Easter–Sep)*

Gorges de la Nesque
Second only to the Verdon gorges *(see pp10–11)* in dramatic potential, the Nesque gorges run for 20 km (12 miles) between the villages of Villes-sur-Auzon and Monieux. The rocky drop descends more than 300 m (1,000 ft), its sides alternately bare or covered in scrub vegetation. Cut into the cliff, the winding road is definitely not for vertigo sufferers. The Castelleras viewpoint looks onto the 850-m (2,800-ft) Rocher de Cire (Wax Rock – so-called because it is home to millions of bees). This is also the start of a

Augustus statue, Orange

Fontaine-de-Vaucluse

testing walk to the bottom of the gorges, where Chapel St-Michel is dug into the rock. ✎ *Map C3*

7 Fontaine-de-Vaucluse

From the base of grandiose, 230-m (750-ft) high cliffs, Europe's most powerful spring pumps out the water which creates the River Sorgue. The romance and mystery of the setting (no one has yet found the exact source of the water) attracts millions of visitors every year, as it once attracted 14th-century Italian poet Petrarch *(see p38)*. Downstream of the source, the charming little village celebrates its most famous inhabitant with a museum in one of the houses claimed to have been his. It also has two excellent museums; about World War II and the other

on speleology (caves and caving).

✎ *Map C3 • Pétrarch Library Museum: Rive gauche de la Sorgue; Open May–mid-Nov: Wed–Mon; Adm • Museum d'Histoire: Chemin du Gouffre; Open Apr–mid-Nov: Wed–Mon; mid-Nov–Dec, Mar: Sat–Sun; DA; Adm • Speleology Museum: Chemin du Gouffre, Open Feb–mid-Nov: daily; DA, Adm*

8 Les Dentelles de Montmirail

Probably the prettiest mountain range in Provence, the Dentelles are formed by three ridges of chalk topped by ragged crests. The French think of these as lacework *(dentelles)*, but they can look more like fangs in rough weather. Within the range, tiny villages (Suzette, La Roque Alric) cling to the crags as if by magic and climbers are attracted to the sheer rock-faces. The walking, too, is spectacularly good, notably up to St Amand, at 730 m (2,400 ft), the highest point. Round the western edge cluster the picturesque wine villages of Beaumes-de-Venise, Gigondas, Vacqueyras and Séguret. It's advisable to stop here after, rather than before, a ramble *(see pp52–3)*. ✎ *Map C2*

The Vaudois Massacre

The bloodiest tale in Provençal history took place in Vaucluse in 1545, when Catholic Royal authorities determined to exterminate early Protestant settlers, the Vaudois. Within weeks as many as 3,000 were dead: women and children were burned alive and villages were destroyed. The memories, and ruins, still haunt the remoter mountainsides.

---

9 Synagogue, Carpentras

Expelled from France in the 14th century, the Jews sought refuge in those parts of Provence then belonging to the pope. This included Carpentras, whose synagogue, founded in 1367, is the oldest still functioning on French soil. Rebuilt in the 18th century, the synagogue looks like neighbouring buildings from the outside: laws forbade decoration.

Within, the ground floor and cellar boasts the old bakery (for unleavened bread) and pools essential for Jewish rituals. A monumental staircase leads to the sumptuous two-storey area of worship (men upstairs, women below), setting for the tabernacle, teba, candelabra and magnificent chandeliers. ✆ *Pl Maurice Charretier • Map C3 • Open 10am–noon, 3–5pm Mon–Fri (to 4pm Fri) • Closed during religious services • Donation*

Cathédrale St-Anne, Apt
The relics of St Anne (mother of the Virgin) were discovered on this site in 776, and here they remain, having survived the destruction of the church and its rebuilding from the 11th century on. The two crypts have also survived, containing sarcophagi from early Christian times. The cathedral has 18th-century paintings and a 15th-century stained-glass window of the Tree of Jesse. The 17th-century St Anne Chapel contains what is said to be the saint's veil, although it's probably of 9th-century Egyptian origin. ✆ *Rue St-Anne • Map C3 • Open 9am–noon, 2:30–6pm Mon–Fri (except during religious ceremonies), 2:30–6pm Sun • Free*

Vaucluse vineyards

A Day's Drive in the Vaucluse Mountains

Morning

Start in Carpentras by visiting the **synagogue**. Take the D942 to Mazan and on, through woodland, to Villes-sur-Auzon, a charming Provençal village. Continue on the D942 to the **Gorges de la Nesque** *(see p117)* to experience 20 km (12 miles) of awe-inspiring scenery, with sheer drops of 300 m (1,000 ft). Pause at the Belvédère de Castelleras for heart-stopping views.

Continue to Monieux, stopping at Les Lavandes restaurant in the village centre *(04 90 64 05 08 • €)* if it is time for lunch and you fancy savoury, rustic cooking. Continue to **Sault** *(see p54)* where, in July and August, the valley is a riot of purple lavender, yellow broom and the white of the rocks – an unmissable sight.

Afternoon

Take the D164 towards **Mont Ventoux** *(see p117)*, another challenging drive, and stop for breaks at Col des Tempêtes for the views across Toulourenc Valley, then the summit for the most stunning panorama in Provence.

Descend the mountain to Malaucène, taking the tiny D90 into the **Dentelles de Montmirail**. Pause in any of the cafés in Beaumes-de-Venise for a glass of the local sweet white wine. Continue to delightful **Séguret** *(see p39)*, then return by the D7 to Carpentras, rewarding yourself with dinner at Le Mesclun *(rue des Poternes. 04 90 46 93 43 • €€)*, the best restaurant in town.

Following pages St-Paul-de-Vence

119

Left **Place de l'Horloge** Right **Vièrge de Pitié, Musée du Petit Palais**

🔟 Avignon Sights

Palais des Papes
The medieval papal palace dominates the town *(see pp8–9)*.

Cathédrale Notre-Dame-des-Doms
The medieval popes' cathedral has 17th-century alterations but a 13th-century altar. ◈ *Pl du Palais • Map B3 • Open 8am–6pm daily (7am–7pm summer)*

Pont St-Bénézet
This 13th-century bridge once had 22 arches, now it has just 4 *(see p60)*. ◈ *Rue Ferruce • Map B3 • Open daily. Mar–Oct: 9am–7pm (to 6:30pm 1–14 Mar; to 8pm Jul; to 8:30pm Aug); 1–15 Sep; Nov–Feb: 9:30am–5:45pm • Adm*

Musée Calvet
This is a fine museum, with collections from ancient Greece to the 20th century. ◈ *65 rue Joseph Vernet • Map B3 • Open 10am–1pm, 2–6pm Wed–Mon • Closed 1 Jan, 1 May, 25 Dec • www.musee-calvet.org • Adm*

Gardens, Cathédrale Notre-Dame-des-Doms

Rue des Teinturiers
This tiny street – formerly home to dye-workers – now buzzes with arty cafés. ◈ *Map B3*

Place de l'Horloge
Built on the old forum, the city's nerve centre is fringed with restaurants, bars and the 19th-century town hall. ◈ *Map B3*

Musée Angladon-Dubrujeaud
This private collection has works by Cézanne, Manet, Picasso and Van Gogh. ◈ *5 rue Laboureur • Map B3 • Open 1–6pm Wed–Sun (also Tue in summer) • Closed 1 Jan, 25 Dec • Adm*

Musée du Petit Palais
This superb collection of medieval and Renaissance art includes early works by Botticelli. ◈ *Pl du Palais • Map B3 • Open 10am–1pm, 2–6pm Wed–Mon • Closed 1 Jan, 1 May, 14 Jul, 1 Nov, 25 Dec • Adm*

Chartreuse du Val-de-Bénédiction
An impressive monastery and chapel with elegant gardens. ◈ *58 rue de la République • Map B3 • Open Apr–Sep: 9:30am–6:30pm daily (Jul: 9am–6:30pm; Aug: 9am–7:30pm); Oct–Mar: 9am–5pm daily • Closed 1 Jan, 1 May, 1 & 11 Nov, 25 Dec • Adm*

Collection Lambert
Avignon's premier showcase for contemporary art. ◈ *Musée d'Art Contemporain, 5 rue Violette • Map B3 • Open 11am–6pm Tue–Sun (to 7pm daily Jul–Aug) • Adm*

Left **Gordes** Right **Château d'Ansouis, Ansouis**

Vaucluse Villages

Roussillon
Ochre mining and erosion have fashioned the multicoloured earth into cliffs and fantastic shapes, creating a bewitching setting for a romantic perched village *(see p38)*. ◈ *Map C3*

Séguret
This remarkable medieval settlement hugs its hillside like a tight belt *(see p39)*. ◈ *Map C3*

Gordes
Fashionable folk flock here, and no wonder. The village is perched above the Coulon Valley, and its little houses appear piled on top of one another. In the centre, the chateau oversees the whole with Renaissance dignity. ◈ *Map C3 • www.gordes-village.com*

Oppède-le-Vieux
Flourishing in Renaissance times, Oppède was deserted by 1900 – no one wanted to live on a barely accessible rock. Now some of the houses are being restored but the spot remains profoundly atmospheric, with medieval castle ruins. ◈ *Map C3*

Brantes
Overhanging the gorges 550 m (1,800 ft) below, Brantes stares across the Toulourenc Valley to Mont Ventoux. Its tiny paved streets and vaulted passages boast a chapel but no shops. It is particularly impressive in March, when the almond trees are in bloom. ◈ *Map C2*

Ansouis
This village, with its wandering little streets, is made truly remarkable by its chateau, built in the 1100s and lived in by the same family until the early 2000s. The vaulted rooms, salons, armoury and kitchens are extraordinary, as are the gardens *(see p47)*. ◈ *Map C3 • Chateau: Call 04 90 77 23 36 for information on tours; Adm*

Ménerbes
Ménerbes was superbly sited for defence. As a Protestant stronghold, it held out for five years during the 16th-century Wars of Religion. The position remains dramatic, but peace now reigns around the citadel and townhouses. The views are terrific. ◈ *Map C3*

Malaucène
This was where Pope Clement V had his summer residence, and it remains a graceful spot of 17th- and 18th-century houses, fountains and avenues shaded by plane trees. ◈ *Map C3*

Vacqueyras
One of Provence's most prestigious wine villages. Note the 11th-century church with its elegant belltower, then go to taste the wine. ◈ *Map C3*

Le Barroux
An eagle's nest of a village, its narrow streets lead steeply up to the splendid chateau at the top. ◈ *Map C3*

For Provence's Top 10 villages **See pp38–9**

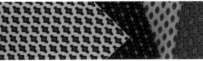

Left **L'Isle-sur-la-Sorgue** Right **Printed fabrics, Les Olivades**

🔟 Shops in Vaucluse

1 L'Isle-sur-la-Sorgue
Not one shop but more than 200 make this little town France's most important antiques and second-hand centre after Paris. Grouped into seven centres, most are open Saturday to Monday, with a market on Sunday mornings. Antiques fairs at Easter and around 15 August. ◈ *Map C3*

2 Farmers' Market, Velleron
Provence isn't short of food markets, but this one is special. It's held in the evening and stallholders must sell homegrown or raised produce only. Monday to Saturday from 6pm, April to September and Tuesday, Wednesday, Friday and Saturday from 4:30pm the rest of the year. ◈ *Map C3*

3 Les Olivades, Avignon
The company has been producing and printing Provençal fabrics since 1818. It's now the only such outfit in the region, with materials, table linen and wedding gowns. ◈ *56 rue Joseph Vermet • Map B3*

4 Vin, Chocolate & Cie, Châteauneuf-du-Pape
An unpromising looking warehouse, but the chocolate wizardry within is dazzling. Enter only if you have iron self-control. ◈ *Rte d'Avignon • Map B3*

5 Les Délices du Luberon, L'Isle-sur-la-Sorgue
Another warehouse and full, this time, of olives, olive preparations and olive derivatives such as tapenade or *melet* (fennel, peppers, olives and anchovies). ◈ *1 ave des Partage des Eaux • Map C3*

6 Edith Mézard, Lumières Goult
The little chateau near Goult provides a perfect setting for beautifully embroidered clothes and a great range of linen for the house. ◈ *Château de l'Ange • Map C3*

7 Confiserie Artisanale Denis Ceccon, Apt
Apt is the proud world capital of crystallized fruit, and Denis Ceccon is one of the few remaining artisans to work by traditional methods – try his apricots. ◈ *60 quai de la Liberté • Map C3*

8 Lou Canesteou, Vaison-la-Romaine
Josiane Déal personally selects the 160 varieties of artisanal cheese for her shop, and has been named a *Meilleur Ouvrier* ("Master of her Craft") for her expertise. ◈ *10 rue Raspail • Map C2*

9 Silvain Frères, St Didier
This is a farming and fruit-growing family also known for their own delicious nougat. Their honey shouldn't be missed. ◈ *Rte de Vénasque St Didier • Map C3*

10 Château Pesquié, Mormoiron
The chateau has lovely grounds and first-rate Ventoux wines. ◈ *Rte de Flassan • Map C2*

Above **La Bastide de Capelongue, Bonnieux**

Price Categories

For a three-course meal for one with half a bottle of wine (or equivalent meal), taxes and extra charges.	€ under €30
	€€ €30–€40
	€€€ €40–€50
	€€€€ €50–€60
	€€€€€ over €60

🔟 Places to Eat

1 La Bastide de Capelongue, Bonnieux

Chef Edouard Loubet is known for aromatic Provençale cuisine – he picks his own herbs for dishes such as rack of lamb smoked with wild thyme. ✆ *Rue du Temple • Map C3 • 04 90 75 89 78 • Closed mid-Jan–mid-Feb, mid-Nov–mid-Dec • €€€€€*

2 Café des Fleurs, L'Isle-sur-la-Sorgue

Delicious Provençal food served in a stylish dining room or on a shady patio. Reserve for Sundays when the town has a busy market. ✆ *9 rue Théodore Aubanel • Map C3 • 04 90 20 66 94 • Closed Tue, Wed (not mid-Jun–Aug), Jan • DA • €€€€*

3 Christian Etienne, Avignon

Frescoes, a terrace and a great way with Provençal fare – notably truffles and tomatoes. ✆ *10 rue de Mons • Map B3 • 04 90 86 16 50 • Closed Sun, Mon (exc Jul) • €€€€€*

4 Auberge de la Fenière, Lourmarin

Reine Sammut, one of France's rare female top chefs, brings international influence to regional cuisine. ✆ *Rte de Cadenet • Map C3 • 04 90 68 11 79 • Closed Mon, Tue (Jul & Aug: open D), mid-Nov–Mar • DA • €€€€*

5 Auberge du Beaucet, Le Beaucet

The hamlet is remote but the refined Provençal cooking is a treat – try the snail ravioli. Booking essential. ✆ *Map C3 • 04 90 66 10 82 • Closed Sun D–Tue L, Dec–Jan • €€€*

6 Le Prieuré, Villeneuve-les-Avignon

The locally sourced menu changes four times a week, offering gastronomic cuisine in a celestial setting. ✆ *7 pl de Chapitre • Map B3 • 04 90 15 90 15 • Closed Mon (low season), Nov–mid-Mar • DA • €€€€€*

7 Hiely-Lucullus, Avignon

One of Avignon's oldest restaurants, yet with a lightness of touch to its classic dishes. ✆ *5 rue de la République • Map B3 • 04 90 86 17 07 • Closed Wed, Thu L, Sat L • €€€€*

8 Les Florets, Gigondas

The panoramic terrace of this hotel-restaurant has superb views of the Dentelles de Montmirail. The regional cuisine is complemented by a fine wine list. Booking is recommended. ✆ *Rte des Dentelles • Map B2 • 04 90 65 85 01 • Closed Wed, Mar • €€€€*

9 Moulin à Huile, Vaison-la-Romaine

Superb setting in the medieval part of town. The excellent Provençal cooking is of a standard to match. ✆ *1 quai du Maréchal Foch • Map C2 • 04 90 36 20 67 • Closed Sun D, Mon • €€€€€*

10 La Fourchette, Avignon

Much favoured by Avignon folk for its country inn style and treatment of Provençale classics, like *boeuf en daube (see p51)*. ✆ *17 rue Racine • Map B3 • 04 90 85 20 93 • Closed Sat, Sun, 3 wks Aug • €€*

Note: *Unless otherwise stated, all restaurants accept credit cards and serve vegetarian meals*

STREETSMART

PROVENCE'S TOP 10

Left **Nice Côte d'Azur airport** Right **Provençal motorway**

🔟 Getting to Provence

1 Flying to Nice

Nice Côte d'Azur Airport is the best gateway for Nice, eastern Provence and the Côte d'Azur and Monaco, with frequent flights from Paris, London, New York and other major cities. Flight times are around 2 hours from the UK, 1 hour from Paris and 9 from New York. The airport is 7 km (4.5 miles) west of Nice and 17 km (10.5 miles) west of Antibes. Buses to Nice bus and railway stations run every 10 minutes. A taxi to the centre costs around €25. There are buses every 35 minutes to Antibes, every hour to Cannes, and every 90 minutes to Monaco. Most international flights use the east terminal; domestic flights use the west terminal. ◎ *Airport information: 08 20 42 33 33, www.nice.aeroport.fr*

2 Flying to Marseille

Marignane (Marseille-Provence) Airport has a terminal for budget airlines, MP2. The airport is handy for Aix, Avignon and Marseille itself, at just 25 km (17 miles) northwest of the city centre and 24 km (15 miles) southeast of Aix. Buses run to Marseille-St Charles railway station every 20 minutes. Taxis to the centre cost around €45. ◎ *Airport information: 04 42 14 14 14, www.marseille. aeroport.fr; mp2.aeroport.fr*

3 Flying to Nîmes

Nîmes, just beyond Provence's western border, is the landing place for cheap charter flights and is a good gateway for Provence, particularly the Camargue, Bouches-du-Rhône, Arles or Avignon. The airport is 15 km (9 miles) southeast of the city, with regular buses. Taxis into Nîmes cost around €25. ◎ *Airport information: 04 66 70 49 49, www.nimes-aeroport.fr*

4 Fly-drive

Packages which involve a flight and a hire car, available from airlines and tour operators, can be cheaper than taking your own car. However, main car rental companies have desks at Marseille and Nice airports and offices in major towns including Avignon, Nice, Cannes, Marseille, Monaco and St-Tropez.

5 Using the Internet

It is always worth looking online for special offers or better rates when booking travel. All the main airlines and ferry companies have websites. For train travel visit raileurope.com or the SNCF website, www.sncf.com.

6 By Train

The TGV Méditerranée high-speed train takes just three hours to travel between Paris and Marseille, with stops at Avignon and Aix. The journey time to Marseille from London is under 7 hours, including a change from the sub-Channel Eurostar service to TGV in Lille.

7 Auto-Train

With this service, your vehicle is checked onto an overnight car-carrying train, while you travel on the train of your choice, paying a normal fare. You collect your car from its destination the next day. Destinations from Paris include Avignon, Toulon, Marseille, Fréjus and Nice. ◎ *http://autotrain. voyages-sncf.com*

8 By Road

Avignon, gateway to Provence by road, is around 1,000 km (640 miles) from the Channel ports. The fastest drive, via France's Autoroute du Soleil, takes around 9 hours and costs around €70 in tolls. Avoiding toll motorways *(péages)* lengthens the journey time by 6 hours.

9 By River

The most romantic and stress-free way to arrive in Provence is on a Rhône river cruiser. Many cruise lines operate luxury, full-board river cruises between Lyon and Avignon.

10 Celebrity-style

Helicopter flights from Nice to Monaco and Cannes are quite affordable, and an exciting way to start your holiday.

Above **Boats moored in St-Tropez**

TOP 10 Getting Around Provence

1 Car Rental
Renting a car on arrival can be cheaper than driving your own car. Other advantages include left-hand drive and replacement vehicles if the one you rent breaks down. Packages combining flights, car rental and accommodation can be very good value, or you can rent a vehicle for part of your stay from major rental companies at airports or in all main towns and resorts. Most car rental companies require drivers to be over 21 with a clean record.

2 By car
If travelling from elsewhere in Europe, using your own car has its advantages: you can bring more luggage, see more of France, and take home more souvenirs. You must have adequate insurance cover and French law also requires modifications to headlights and a range of accessories including fire extinguisher, replacement bulb set, warning triangle, reflective vest and first-aid kit. Emergency breakdown insurance is also advisable: consult your insurer or motoring organization.

3 Taxis
Taxis are reliable and use meters *(compteurs)* but are not usually flagged down on the street – find one at a taxi rank, book by phone, or ask your hotel or restaurant to call one.

4 City Transport
France has some of the best public transport in Europe and getting around the region's major cities by bus, tram and (in Marseille) metro presents few problems. Fares are integrated, so a single ticket can be used on any combination of transport for one hour. Day passes and books of tickets *(carnets)* are also available *(see p135)*.

5 By Train
From Marseille, rail lines run west to Arles and Nîmes, north to Aix and Avignon and east to Nice and Monaco. TER (regional express trains) operate an inland route from Nice to Digne-les-Bains. Several discounts are available *(see p135)*.

6 Inter-city Bus
Inter-city buses supplement trains between major cities. Numerous companies operate from long-distance bus stations *(gares routières)* in cities and larger towns. Smaller villages and rural towns are poorly served by buses, many villages having no service at all.

7 Cycling
Cycling is a great way to explore Provence. Mountainous regions may be only for the super-fit, but there are gentler rides in the lowlands, along the coast and in the dead-flat Camargue. Mountain bikes *(velos tous terrains* or *VTT)* can be hired in all major towns and resorts (tourist offices have lists) and marked cycle trails range from demanding to totally relaxed *(see p57)*. Eco-friendly free cycle schemes, like Vélo in Marseille, are springing up in towns across the region. Tourist offices have up-to-date details.

8 Walking Trails
Provence is superb walking country, offering guided or marked walks through historic cities and coastal paths, *sentiers balisés* (local trails) and *sentiers de grande randonnée* (long-distance hiking tracks), part of a network that crosses France. Main long-distance trails are the GR5, GR51 GR6 and GR9. Maps and guides are available from tourist offices *(see p57)*.

9 On Horseback
Horses can be hired by the day or for longer, with or without a guide, on gentle or more demanding trails. The Camargue is ideal riding country *(see pp20–21)*.

10 Yachts and Cruisers
The Riviera is prime sailing country and every kind of vessel, from small yachts and catamarans to fully crewed motor-cruisers, can be chartered out of marinas including Nice, Cannes, St-Tropez, Antibes and St-Jean.

Above **Provençal tourist office**

🔟 Sources of Information

1 Tourist Offices
Information on sights, events, travel and places to stay is available from many sources including the French national tourist office (with offices abroad), regional and city tourist offices and, in villages, the local *Syndicat d'Initiative*. You'll also find information desks at airports and main railway stations *(see p128)*. Guides and maps are available in English and other major European languages.

2 Government Tourist Offices
The French Government Tourist Office (Maison de la France) is a one-stop shop for information on how to get to Provence, what to see and where to stay *(see box)*.

3 Comité Régional du Tourisme
The Regional Committee for Tourism for Provence-Alpes-Côte d'Azur is based in Marseille, with multilingual maps, guides and a hotel finding and booking service. The tourist office of the Bouches-du-Rhône is also based in Marseille. ⊗ *Comité Régional du Tourisme Provence-Alpes-Côte d'Azur: 61 La Canebière, Marseille; Map C5, 04 91 56 47 00; www. decouverte-paca.fr* • *CDT Bouches-du-Rhône: 13 rue Roux de Brignoles, Marseille; 04 91 13 84 13; www.visitprovence.com*

4 Cannes Tourist Office
The main information source for Cannes and the Côte d'Azur is in the town centre. The website will help you plan your trip. ⊗ *Palais des Festivals, La Croisette, BP 272, Cannes* • *Map G4* • *04 92 99 84 22* • *www.cannes-destination.fr*

5 Nice Tourist Office
This should be your first stop in town for maps, accommodation advice and information on what's on in Nice. ⊗ *5 promenade des Anglais, 06000 Nice* • *Map H4* • *08 92 70 74 07* • *www.nicetourism.com*

6 Alpes-Maritimes Tourist Office
For information on where to stay and what to do in Nice's hinterland contact the Comité Regionale du Tourisme. ⊗ *455 promenade des Anglais, Nice* • *Map H4* • *04 93 37 78 78* • *www. cotedazur-tourisme.com*

7 Monaco Tourist Office
Practical information on all aspects of travel in the area is available from the Monaco Direction du Tourisme de la Principauté de Monaco. ⊗ *2a blvd des Moulins, Monte Carlo* • *Map H4* • *00 377 92 166 116* • *www.visit monaco.com*

8 Alpes-de-Haute-Provence Tourist Office
For wide-ranging travel information on the Alpes de Haute Provence, visit the tourist office in Digne-les-Baines. ⊗ *8 rue Bad-Mergentheim, Digne-les-Bains* • *Map E2* • *04 92 31 57 29* • *www.alpes-haute-provence.com*

9 Var Tourist Office
The main information source for visitors to the Var region. ⊗ *1 blvd de Strasbourg, Toulon* • *Map F4* • *04 94 18 59 60* • *www.visitvar.fr*

10 Vaucluse Tourist Office
The Vaucluse office is based in Avignon, and has a useful website. ⊗ *12 rue Collège de la Croix, BP 147, Avignon* • *Map B3* • *04 90 80 47 00* • *www. provenceguide.com*

French Government Tourist Offices

Australia
25 Bligh St, Level 13, Sydney NSW 2000 • *02 9231 5244* • *http://au.franceguide.com*

France
79–81 rue Clichy, 79009 Paris • *01 42 96 70 00*

United Kingdom
300 High Holborn, London WC1V 7JH • *090 6824 4123* • *http://uk.franceguide.com*

USA
825 Third Ave, 29th floor, New York, NY 10022 • *212 838 7800* • *http://us.franceguide.com*

Left **August crowds** Right **Forest fire warning sign**

ATTENTION AU FEU

TOP 10 Things to Avoid

1 Autoroutes in August

French *autoroutes* (motorways) are very crowded in August, especially during the first and last weekends of the month, when huge numbers of holiday-makers from northern France head at top speed for the sunny south. There are long traffic jams and often serious accidents. Avoid driving south at these times if possible.

2 Cannes Film Festival

For two weeks in May it becomes impossible to find a hotel room or a table at a good restaurant in Cannes as the resort is overrun with up to 30,000 film stars and their entourages, directors, producers, financiers, journalists and other hangers-on. This is strictly an insider's event, and unless you have Hollywood ambitions, give Cannes a wide berth during the festival *(see p58).*

3 Monte Carlo Rally and Monaco Grand Prix

Monaco is host to two of the world's most prestigious motor sports events, the Rallye Monte Carlo every January and the Monaco Grand Prix, at differing dates during the Grand Prix season *(see p59).* Both are worth avoiding – it's claimed that to be sure of a room during either event it is

necessary to book 10 years ahead. Both events take place through the city streets, so much of Monaco is closed off.

4 Bullfights

The traditional Provençal bullfight *(course à la cocarde)* is a bloodless affair in which the bullfighter *(razeteur)* tries to snatch a red ribbon *(cocarde)* from the horns of an increasingly irritated bull. In the arenas of Arles and Nîmes, however, Spanish-style *corridas,* in and then killed, are often part of the entertainment. These are advertised as *mise à mort* (to the death).

5 Motoring Offences

Police issue heavy fines on the spot for speeding and for other motoring offences. The blood alcohol limit for drink-driving is low: one glass of wine or a 33cl bottle of beer will take you close to the limit, two will exceed it. Drivers can pay fines by credit card, by phone, or on the Internet.

6 Dangerous Drivers

After Greece and Portugal, France has the worst road accident record in the EU. Many French motorists drive aggressively, overtake carelessly and ignore safe braking distances on motorways. Expect the unexpected at all times.

7 Hotel Telephones

Many hotels charge very high rates for international phone calls. It is far cheaper to call from a post office or telephone booth using a credit card or phonecard *(see p138).*

8 Cheap Wine

With the cheapest *vins de France* (local wines) costing as little as €4 for a five-litre plastic flagon, there is a strong temptation to look no further. Many of these wines are quite drinkable but some are guaranteed to produce a crippling hangover. For a few euros more, France has far better wines to offer.

9 Lighting Fires

The South of France has a serious forest fire problem in July and August, when undergrowth and pine forests are tinder dry. High risk areas are closed from the beginning of July to mid-September, and lighting camp fires anywhere in the region is strictly forbidden.

10 Hurrying

It takes a little time to adapt to the relaxed pace of Provence, but there is little point in rushing things. Almost everything closes for lunch between noon and 3pm. As the Provençal proverb goes: "Slow in the mornings, and not too fast in the afternoons."

Left **Gîtes de France logo** Centre **Typical chateau hotel** Right **Hotel doorman**

🔟 Accommodation Tips

1 High and Low Season

Don't even think about visiting Provence in high season without reserving accommodation. From the beginning of July to the end of August the region, especially the Riviera and Côte d'Azur, is at its busiest and everything, from grand hotels to camp sites, is full. May to mid-June and September to mid-October are less crowded. Some smaller hotels in rural areas close from November to February.

2 How to Book

You can book direct with hotels and other accommodation providers by phone, fax and, increasingly, by email and via the web. The French Government tourist office website provides useful links for finding and booking accommodation. You will normally be asked for a deposit, which you can pay by credit card in most larger hotels and camp sites, or by money order.

3 Families

The South of France is very well geared up for family tourism, both on the coast and inland. Many hotels will provide an extra bed for smaller children or a cot for babies at a nominal cost. Gîtes (see p146) and camp sites (see p145) also offer excellent value for families travelling on a budget. Most camp sites have facilities and activities for children.

4 On a Budget

The best way to save money is to travel off-season (and avoid the glitzy Riviera resorts). However, accommodation in France can be surprisingly cheap, with rooms in small pensions available for as little as €35 for a double room (see p144). In off-season periods, ask for special offers and discounts, such as three nights for the price of two. Even hotels on the Côte d'Azur have special offers out of season.

5 Camping

Camp sites in Provence usually feature pools, playgrounds, café-bar and often a mini-market and morning bread delivery. They become crowded in July and August, and most close their gates by 10pm. Independent camping is discouraged, as is sleeping on beaches.

6 Hotel Chains

France pioneered the "limited service hotel" which offers clean, comfortable rooms at budget prices, and not much else. Chains such as Formule 1, Campanile, Etap and others cluster at motorway junctions, airports and on the out-skirts of cities. Although lacking in character they

can be perfect for the first and last night of your stay.

7 Self-catering

Accommodation in gîtes is plentiful – most are privately owned and often in pretty cottages or farmhouses. Crockery and kitchen utensils are supplied, but you usually have to bring your own bedlinen and do your own cleaning.

8 Villas

A villa holiday offers a more luxurious version of self-catering. Most villas are in or near coastal resorts and usually have a pool. They offer basic maid service (cleaning and linen change) but the more luxurious can be fully staffed with cook, valet service and chauffeur.

9 Apartments

Holiday apartments can be found in most resort areas, especially in the Cannes-Antibes area, but few offer the facilities of a gîte or villa and most are geared to long stays.

10 Yachts and Cruisers

You don't have to be mega-rich to stay on a yacht or cruiser. The closer you get to Cannes or Antibes the more expensive such boats become, but there are less ostentatious vessels in such harbours as Le Lavandou and Ste-Maxime.

For accommodation recommendations See pp140–47

Left **Charcuterie** and **quincaillerie** in a Provençal village Centre **Fresh salad** Right **Pavement café**

🔟 Eating and Drinking Tips

1 Cafés and Bars

There's not much to choose in Provence between establishments calling themselves cafés and those that call themselves bars. All serve alcoholic drinks and coffee all day, and most serve simple snacks such as ham, cheese or salami sandwiches. Village cafés usually close around 8pm but city and resort café-bars stay open much later, some until dawn.

2 Menus

Most restaurants have several set menus, the cheapest usually starting as low as €12. If you are not sure what to order, these menus are excellent value. Eating à la carte (selecting each dish yourself) is usually more expensive.

3 Pichet and Pression

Wine served by the *pichet* (jug) – usually the local *vin de France*, bought by the barrel and decanted – is normally much cheaper than wine by the glass or bottle, and always palatable. If you want a draught beer, ask for *une pression*; if you order *"une bière"* you will be served a more expensive, bottled beer.

4 Picnics

The Provençaux, like all French people, love picnics, and when you plan an *al fresco* lunch at the beach or in the country you will be spoilt for choice. *Boulangeries* (bakeries) and *pâtisseries* (pastry shops) sell a wonderful choice of loaves, rolls and pastries and most *boulangeries* sell delicious ready-made sandwiches. Provence's typical takeaway snack is the *pan bagnat*, a crusty roll soaked in olive oil and stuffed with *salade Niçoise (see p51)*. To make your own sandwiches, head for the village *traiteur*, *charcuterie* or supermarket to buy cuts of cold meats, chicken and sausage.

5 Vegetarians

Vegetarians are poorly served in Provençal restaurants. Few offer anything more than salad, omelette or cheese – soups almost always contain meat stock. However, vegetarians catering for themselves will find mouthwatering fresh fruit and vegetables, delicious cheeses, Provençal ingredients such as truffles, olives, pine nuts and garlic and dozens of aromatic herbs.

6 Wine "en vrac"

Throughout Provence signs invite the traveller to visit local wineries *(caves cooperatives)* and enjoy a tasting *(dégustation)*, after which you will be expected to buy at least a bottle. If staying in self-catering accommodation, this is a good opportunity to invest in a *vrac* (plastic barrel) containing five or ten litres of wine, usually at competitive prices.

7 Water

Water as well as wine is always drunk with meals and even in upmarket restaurants it's accepted to ask for a *carafe d'eau* (jug of tap water) rather than a bottle of mineral water.

8 Soft Drinks

Soft drinks are no cheaper than wine or beer. Typical Provençal offerings include a range of sweet cordials with ice and water: mint syrup *(syrop de menthe)*, blackcurrant *(cassis)*, grenadine and tart lemon juice *(citron pressé)*.

9 Bloody, Rare or Well-done

If you like your steak well done, order it *"bien cuit"*, for medium: *"à point"*. For very rare, ask for *"saignant"* (literally, "bleeding") and if you like your steak barely cooked ask for *"bleu"* (blue).

10 Bills and Tipping

In cafés the bill for each drink is brought to your table with your order but there is no need to pay until you leave. A small tip is customary. In restaurants, menu prices almost always include the tip, so an additional gratuity is not expected.

Left **Bags of dried herbs** Right **Provençal olive seller**

🔟 Shopping Tips

Tax and Allowances
If you live within the EU you can take home as much wine, spirits, tobacco and perfume as you wish, although if you are travelling by air you are unlikely to be able to find room in your weight allowance for more than two bottles of wine or spirits. If you live outside the EU you are limited to two bottles. Non-EU residents can claim back the value added tax (TVA) included in the sales price on purchases worth more than €180 in one shop, to be exported within three months.

Wine
For wine to take home, the world-class appellations of the Côtes du Rhône, and especially those of Châteauneuf-du-Pape *(see p53)*, are the best investment. You can buy them young to drink straight away, or let them age for up to seven years for a long-lasting souvenir.

Herbs
Bunches of oregano and thyme can be bought in markets or in packaged form in supermarkets – they will add the scents and flavours of the south to your kitchen long after you reach home. They make attractive gifts too, as do bags of dried lavender packed in local fabrics, but check your home country's rules on importing foodstuffs.

Truffles
Truffles must be the ultimate high-value, low-weight souvenir or gift to take home. Taking up next to no space in your luggage, the "black diamonds" from the Vaucluse cost as much as €180 per kilogram, so there's no risk of buying too many. Best places to buy include Puyméras, Richerenches and Valréas, all in the Vaucluse region *(see p51)*.

Olives, Olive Oil and Olivewood
Nothing, perhaps, is more typical of Provence than the olive tree and its fruit. For happy memories of meals in the sun, take home virgin olive oil – the best is said to come from around Nyons, in the Vaucluse, or from the Vallée des Baux olive groves of the Alpilles region. Or you could buy a jar of green olives with Provençal herbs, bars of savon de Marseille olive oil soap, or attractive, practical salad bowls, forks and salad spoons carved from close-grained olivewood.

Cheese
The French gift for presentation makes local produce irresistible (as it's intended to). Make one last visit to a market or *épicier* (grocer) to fill your basket with goat's cheese wrapped in chestnut leaves or numerous other fabulous options.

Santon Figures
Santons ("little saints") were originally designed to decorate Nativity scenes at Christmas but these pottery figures make unique Provençal mementos and gifts. There are dozens of different figures, each representing a traditional trade or skill. hey can be found all over the region, but are especially popular in Marseille.

Perfume
Perfumed oils, lavender water or orange water, and bubble baths and shampoos scented with different fragrances can be found on the shelves of Provence's many fine perfumiers.

Museum Prints
Museum-quality reproductions of works by the masters who have lived in Provence *(see pp36–7)* are on sale at gallery shops attached to the region's leading museums of art *(see pp34–5)*. Weighing very little and rolling up into a conveniently small package, unframed prints are excellent purchases to take home.

Confectionery
As gifts, Provençal confectionery such as *calissons*, the almond-paste sweetmeats from Aix, are perfect, as are *marrons glacés*, and preserved lemons, figs and other fruits.

Left **French Riviera Pass** Right **Student ID card**

🔟 Provence on a Budget

1 Off-season Travel

During July and August, when Provence throngs with thousands of French and foreign holidaymakers, the price of everything, from a beach deckchair to a hotel room, is highest. Provence is much cheaper (and more pleasant) in May and June and in September and October.

2 Carnets

Buying a *carnet* of five or ten tickets from bus and railway stations for public transport in larger towns such as Marseille, Nice and Monaco is cheaper and more convenient than buying single tickets.

3 Discounts

Many museums and attractions offer discounted admission to students, over-60s and families of five or more. Admission to state-owned museums and monuments is free for under-26s resident in the EU. ID is required.

4 Rail Passes

French Railways (SNCF) offer the France Railpass, which is hard to beat for flexibility and value for money. It allows from three to nine days travel on any route, from high-speed TGVs *(see p129)* to mountain railways, anywhere in France within one month. The Senior France Railpass is for people over 60. Both passes are available at all major French stations, but can also be booked via travel agents before you leave home. For more information, see www.eurorailways.com or www.europeonrail.com

5 Youth Hostels

Youth hostels can be found in Marseille, Nice, Menton, St-Raphaël, Aix and Arles, and at several national parks. Despite the name, there is no age limit for travellers. For more information contact the Fédération Unie des Auberges de Jeunesse (FUAJ) in Paris.
🕾 *FUAJ: 01 44 89 87 27*
• *www.fuaj.org*

6 No-Frills Airlines

British-based budget airlines flying to Provence from the UK include Ryanair to Nîmes and Toulon; easyJet, Jet2 and flybe to Nice; and Jet2 and flybe to Avignon. Ryanair and easyJet also fly to Marseille's MP2 terminal. 🕾 *Ryanair: www.ryanair.com*
• *easyJet: www.easyjet. com* • *flybe: www.flybe. com* • *Jet2: www.Jet2.com*

7 Museum Cards

Multi-site and multiple entry passes for local sights and museums include *Avignon Passion*, *Arles Passeports* and the *French Riviera Pass*, which are available from www.fnacspectacles. com, through local tourist offices *(see p130)* and at museums. With the region's great choice of museums and historic monuments to visit, these passes often result in considerable savings.

8 Camping

Provençal camp sites can be quite lavish affairs, with swimming pools, self-service laundry, mini-market and restaurant and are good value, but are not always cheaper than simple hotels *(see p144)*.

9 Working Holidays

Grape-picking is hard work and although pickers *(vendangeurs)* usually receive lunch and dinner daily as well as their pay, accommodation is not always part of the deal. The *vendange* (harvest) in Provence is from mid-September to mid-October. Recruiting starts as early as May, and the best way to find work is to call or write directly to as many *domaines* (estates) as possible. Lists of wine growers who recruit foreign workers are available from local tourist offices.

10 Hitch-hiking

Hitch-hiking is permitted on all roads except *autoroutes* (motorways), and in some rural areas is the only cheap alternative to infrequent village buses. Use caution: women are advised not to hitch-hike solo and travel after dark is also not advisable.

➤ *For value for money accommodation* **See p145**

Left **Camp site accommodation** Right **Provence beach**

Tips for Families

1 Hotels

Young children can usually share a room with parents at no extra cost. Hotels such as those in the Campanile and Formule 1 chains *(see p132)*, located at motorway junctions and near major towns and airports, offer family rooms which sleep three to five people for the same price as for two. Many youth hostels also have comfortable family rooms which are ideal for families with older children *(see p135)*.

2 Camp Sites

Camp sites in Provence are very much geared to cater for families, with play areas for children and large discounts for under 12s. Some more expensive camp sites also offer supervised activities for children *(see p145)*.

3 Children's Menus

Children are welcome in almost all restaurants and are not excluded from cafés and bars. Restaurants do not usually provide special facilities for children such as high chairs. Some, especially those in tourist resorts, offer fixed-price menus for children, at around half the price.

4 Activities

Many resorts on the coast, as well as national and regional parks, offer a range of organized activities and events for children during the summer season. A schedule of events is usually available from the local tourist office, to be found even in very small villages *(see p130)*. Many French festival events *(see pp58–9)* culminate in fireworks displays which will delight older children but may terrify toddlers. Children will also enjoy the sound and light shows held throughout the summer season at many castles and other historic buildings.

5 Public Transport

Children are eligible for free or reduced price travel on French Railways (SNCF) trains and buses and on urban public transport. Babies normally travel free.

6 Car Rental

Use of child safety seats and rear seat belts is obligatory under French law. All major car rental companies will provide children's safety seats if requested in advance. There is normally a small charge for this service.

7 On the Beach

Most beaches along the Côte d'Azur and the Riviera are safe for children, with shallow waters, gentle waves and lifeguards on duty in many places. However, sensible precautions should be taken. Babies, toddlers and older children are at risk of sunburn from April to October, and use of high-factor, waterproof sun block is advisable. Beaches become very crowded during July and August, making it easy for toddlers to become separated from parents. On rocky beaches, look out for black sea urchins with spines which give painful stings.

8 Self-catering

Using self-catering accommodation gives parents greater flexibility and allows families to keep to the mealtimes and bedtimes they are accustomed to instead of living by hotel schedules.

9 Motorway Services

French *autoroute* service areas cater very well for parents with babies and small children, with clean, spacious nappy (diaper) changing areas, toddlers' toilets, disposable nappy (diaper) vending machines and baby food on sale in service area shops.

10 Nappies (Diapers) and other Necessities

Remember that French opening hours are much more restrictive than those in the UK. Parents should make sure they have stocks of necessities to last through the long French weekend.

Left **Wheelchair ramp** Right **Outside restaurant tables**

🔟 Tips for Disabled Travellers

① Before You Leave

France is working hard to improve access to all of its services. Before you go it's worth checking out the RADA (the Royal Association for Disability and Rehabilitation) website for general information on disabled and older people travelling abroad. The best source of information on disabled facilities in France is the Association des Paralysés de France (APF), which produces an annual *Guide Vacances* holiday booklet. For advice in English, and a range of other languages, visit the France tourist office website for your own country. ✆ *RADAR: 12 City Forum, 250 City Rd, London, 020 7250 3222, www.radar.org. uk • APF: www.apf.asso.fr*

② Holiday Companies

Access Travel offers wheelchair-accessible properties that have been inspected or suggested by a wheelchair user. They also offer special air fares worldwide and will liaise with airlines to arrange services. The website www.youreable. com offers advice on organizing all aspects of your holiday, as well as specialized holidays for people with disabilities. ✆ *Access Travel: www. access-travel.co.uk*

③ Airports

Under current EU law, airports serving more than 150,000 passengers per year must provide free assistance to disabled passengers. At Nice and Marseille airports, they suggest you notify them 36-hours in advance. ✆ *IDEM Multi Services: 08 20 42 33 33 (Nice); 04 42 14 27 42 (Marseille)*

④ Museums and Galleries

Admission is free to blind people and others in need in most major museums and art galleries in Nice, Avignon and Marseille. Most have audio and Braille guides in English. Some museums also loan wheelchairs.

⑤ Public Transport

Free or reduced rate transport is available in Nice and Marseille for people with disabilities and their carers. SNCF French Railways has introduced the *Accès Plus* service and has an accessibility helpline. For wheelchair access to trains, book 48 hours in advance. SOS Voyageurs offers help to older travellers. ✆ *SNCF helpline: 3635 (say "Access Plus"); SNCF Accès Plus: 08 90 64 06 50 • SOS Voyageurs: 04 93 16 02 61 (Nice); 04 91 62 12 80 (Marseille); www. accessibilite.sncf.com*

⑥ Accommodation

Most mid-priced 2- to 3-star hotels have elevators. Many motel-style hotel chains have wheelchair access direct from the car park. Gîtes de France publishes a guide to accessible farmhouse accommodation available through Maison de la France *(see p130)*. The Association des Paralysés de France has a guide to accessible accommodation (in French), which you can order: *Guide Vacances Fairéface.* ✆ *Association des Paralysés de France: 17 blvd August Blanqui, 75013 Paris, 01 40 78 69 00*

⑦ Restaurants

Most restaurants have poor access for wheelchair users. In summer, picking an outside table eases the problem.

⑧ Loisirs Provence Mediterranée

This company organizes holidays in Provence for disabled adults, mainly in *gîtes.* ✆ *Loisirs Provence Mediterranée: 36 rue St-Jacques, 13006 Marseille, 04 91 04 20 20, www.lpm.asso.fr*

⑨ Specialized Guide

The APF association for people with cerebral palsy publishes a guide to wheelchair accessible accommodation, transport and museums throughout France (in French). *To order the guide: APF, 13 pl Rungis, 75013 Paris, 01 53 80 92 97, www.apf.asso.fr*

⑩ Tourist Office Leaflets

The main tourist offices will have information leaflets on facilities for the disabled *(see p130)*.

NE LAISSEZ PAS UN RHUME VOUS GACHER LA VIE !

Télécarte 50

LA POSTE

Left **French phonecard** Right **Postbox**

Banking and Communication

1 Language and Etiquette

English is widely spoken by people working in coastal resorts, tourist offices, hotels, larger restaurants and airports. It is less fluently spoken in urban Marseille and in rural communities, where you will need a grasp of French in order to understand and be understood. Etiquette is highly valued: shake hands on being introduced and use the titles *"Monsieur"* and *"Madame"* on greeting.

2 Changing Money

Foreign currency and travellers' cheques in all major currencies can be changed into euros at exchange offices and banks. French francs ceased to be legal tender in February 2002. Euro notes are issued in denominations of €5, €10, €20, €50, €100, €200 and €500 and coins in €2, €1, and 50, 20, 10, 5, 2 and 1 cents. Cash and travellers' cheques can be changed at larger post offices. Banks are usually open 9am–noon and 2–5pm Monday to Friday, but some also open on Saturday. You can also change money at larger hotels.

3 Credit and Debit Cards

Cash can be drawn from your bank or credit card account using automatic teller machines (ATMs) in all towns and larger villages. On-screen instructions are in English and French. Credit cards can be used to pay for motorway tolls but smaller shops, restaurants, hotels, camp sites and *gîte* operators prefer cash.

4 Public Phones

International and local calls can be made from telephone booths even in the smallest communities. Some phones accept only French telephone debit cards (*télécartes*), which can be bought from post offices, newsagents and *tabacs* (tobacconists); others accept most credit and debit cards. You can also call from metered telephone booths at larger post offices, or via the *pays direct* service which allows you to place your call through an operator in your home country and pay by credit card, charge card, or reversing the charges.

5 Mobile Phones

Reception is generally good but it may be hard to obtain a signal in deep mountain valleys. UK mobile phones will work in France if they have a roaming facility enabled. North American Mobile phones will only operate in France if they are tri- or quad-band. Always check roaming charges with your service provider before travelling, as making and receiving calls can be expensive. It can be cheaper to buy a French pay as you go sim card.

6 Post Offices

Most post offices open 9am–noon and 2–5pm Monday to Friday and 9am–noon on Saturday. Stamps are sold singly or in books of ten *(carnets)*.

7 Fax and Poste Restante

Faxes can be sent or received at any post office. For a small fee you can also use the *poste restante* service to receive mail at any post office.

8 Internet

There are Internet cafés in all main towns, larger villages and most coastal resorts. Many hotels also offer Wi-Fi connections, although they are not usually free. If you need to use a cable connection be aware that French modem sockets are incompatible with UK and US plugs. You'll either need to buy an adaptor or a French modem lead.

9 Television and Radio

Most hotels subscribe to multilingual cable and satellite channels, which vary the diet of French-language entertainment.

10 Newspapers

The English-language *International Herald Tribune* is available in resorts and at station newsagents in big cities on day of publication. International daily papers usually arrive in resorts the day after publication.

Left **Ambulance** Right **Sunbathers protected by sunscreen**

🔟 Security and Health

1 Emergencies
SOS Médecins, the 24-hour emergency medical service, can send an ambulance, paramedic or a doctor. For most emergencies payment in cash is required immediately after treatment. ✆ *SOS Médecins (Nice): 08 10 85 01 01; for local emergency numbers in Provence, visit www.sosmedecins-france.fr*

2 Travel Insurance
France has excellent health care but treatment is not free. Take out adequate insurance to cover all emergencies – policies are available through your credit card company, bank, motoring association, household insurance company, or direct from insurers. Policies sold by travel agents are more expensive. For EU citizens, the European Health Insurance Card is available from post offices or online; it entitles visitors to free health care but only for basic treatment.

3 Minor Ailments
Provence has no serious health risks. Tap water is safe, but water from village fountains should be drunk only if it bears the sign *"eau potable"*. Sunburn is a risk throughout the summer: wear a hat and sunscreen. In early summer hay fever sufferers should carry antihistamine tablets or drops. Change of diet and climate can cause diarrhoea or indigestion. Remedies are available from pharmacies.

4 Insects and Pests
Mosquitoes are common in summer. Repellents containing deet (diethyltoluamide) and/or citronella oil will keep them away. Plug-in electric repellent pads can be bought at pharmacies. On rocky beaches, beware of treading on spiky sea urchins; when swimming, watch out for stinging jellyfish. Hornets and scorpions, both of which have a painful sting, are harmless unless provoked. You will encounter snakes on country walks, but the only venomous species, the viper, is shy, rarely seen and harmless unless trodden on.

5 Breakdowns and Accidents
A red warning triangle must be placed 50–100 m (160–300 ft) behind any broken down vehicle. In the event of an accident, call the police/emergency services and await their arrival by your car. Anyone who leaves the car must wear a luminous yellow jacket.

6 Doctors
A 24-hour doctor service *(médécin de garde)* operates in major towns. The telephone number is obtainable from your hotel, police stations or pharmacies.

7 Dentists
Dental care services are offered by major hospitals.

8 Hospitals
The accident and emergency clinic *(service des urgences)* of any public hospital will treat injuries and unexpected illnesses. Payment is required immediately.

9 Pharmacies
Pharmacies are indicated by a green cross. French pharmacists are usually helpful in suggesting remedies for minor illnesses. In all towns one pharmacy will open at night and weekends – details are posted on all pharmacy doors.

10 Crime
Theft from cars, bags and luggage is prevalent along the Riviera and Côte d'Azur – do not take valuables, passports, tickets or more cash than you need to the beach. Violent crime is less common, but take the same precautions as you would at home.

> **Emergency Numbers**
>
> **Emergency Services: 112**
>
> **Police: 17**
>
> **Ambulance: 15**
>
> **Fire Brigade: 18**

Left **Carlton InterContinental, Cannes** Right **Hôtel Hermitage, Monte Carlo**

⑩ Grand Hotels

① Le Negresco, Nice
The flagship of the whole Riviera, the Negresco is the grandest of grand hotels, from its splendid *belle époque* façade and public areas to its immaculate rooms and attentive service. One of the world's most opulent hotels. ✆ 37 promenade des Anglais • Map P5 • 04 93 16 64 00 • www.hotel-negresco-nice.com • DA • €€€€€

② Hôtel du Cap Eden Roc, Antibes
As ostentatious as the Negresco in its way, the Eden Roc is another landmark of the Riviera and has been for more than a century. It offers exclusivity and film-star chic in tropical gardens and is, in a word, idyllic. ✆ Blvd Kennedy • Map G4 • 04 93 61 39 01 • www.hotel-du-cap-eden-roc.com • DA • €€€€€

③ Hôtel Hermitage, Monte Carlo
The Hermitage recalls the splendour of *belle époque* Monaco, with its glass-domed atrium, its over-the-top restaurant decorated in pink and gold, marble terrace and fine service. A monument in its own right, it is one of Europe's smartest hotels – a reputation it has retained for more than 100 years. ✆ Sq Beaumarchais • Map H4 • 00 377 98 06 40 00 • www.hotelhermitagemontecarlo.com • DA • €€€€€

④ Hôtel de Paris, Monte Carlo
Rivalling the Hermitage for *belle époque* splendour, the Hôtel de Paris has a famous café-terrace on the ground floor *(see p102)* and is very close to the casino *(see pp26–7)*. Queen Victoria stayed here, as have a host of other crowned heads and celebrities. ✆ Pl du Casino • Map H4 • 00 377 98 06 30 00 • www. hoteldeparismontecarlo. com • DA • €€€€€

⑤ Carlton Inter-Continental, Cannes
The Carlton is a Cannes landmark, home of the stars during the Film Festival and appropriately luxurious, with its private beach and high standards of service. Part of an international chain, it retains an individual character. ✆ 58 La Croisette • Map G4 • 04 93 06 40 06 • www. intercontinental-carlton-cannes.com • DA • €€€€€

⑥ Hôtel Royal Riviera, Jean-Cap-Ferrat
This luxury hotel is situated on a private beach on Cap Ferrat peninsula. The rooms are distributed between the main building and the Orangerie. All are spacious with modern amenities. The restaurant has a terrace and there is a heated pool. ✆ 3 ave Jean Monnet • Map H4 • 04 93 76 31 00 • www.royal-riviera.com • DA • €€€€€

⑦ La Réserve, Beaulieu
Opened in the late 19th century this pink palace in its semi-tropical grounds is a grand place to stay, still retaining the glory of its 1920s heyday. ✆ 5 blvd du Maréchal Leclerc • Map G4 • 04 93 01 00 01 • www.reserve beaulieu.com • DA • €€€€€

⑧ Grand Hôtel Nord-Pinus, Arles
This historic hotel is the best address in Arles. The lounge and foyer have a Provençal atmosphere. ✆ 17 pl du Forum • Map B4 • Closed mid-Nov–mid-Mar • 04 90 93 44 44 • www.nord-pinus.com • DA • €€€

⑨ Hôtel l'Arlatan, Arles
Built in the 16th century, this was the town house of the Counts of Arlatan and is, as a consequence, steeped in history, with a walled garden and Roman relics in the foyer. ✆ 26 rue du Sauvage • Map B4 • 04 90 93 56 66 • Closed mid-Nov–Mar • www.hotel-arlatan.fr • DA • €

⑩ Hôtel d'Europe, Avignon
Step back in time as you enter the ornate gates of this beautiful, historic hotel. Heavy wooden furniture and antique tapestries create an elegant atmosphere. ✆ 12 pl Crillon • Map B3 • 04 90 14 76 76 • www. heurope.com • €€€€€

Note: Unless otherwise stated, all hotels accept credit cards, have en suite bathrooms and air conditioning

Price Categories

For a standard, double room per night (with breakfast if included), taxes and extra charges.

€	under €100
€€	€100–€150
€€€	€150–€250
€€€€	€250–€350
€€€€€	over €350

Above **Monte Carlo Beach Hotel, Roquebrune-Cap-Martin**

🔟 Luxury Resorts

1 La Voile d'Or, St-Jean-Cap-Ferrat

This luxury resort hotel next to the quiet (by Riviera standards) port boasts two saltwater pools and a highly regarded restaurant, as well as lush greenery, romantic terraces and excellent service. 🖎 *7 ave Jean Mermoz • Map G4 • 04 93 01 13 13 • Closed Nov–Apr • www.lavoiledor.fr • €€€€€*

2 Martinez, Cannes

A landmark on Cannes' esplanade, the Martinez is a triumph of *fin-de-siècle* wedding-cake stucco architecture, with a private beach. Part of the Concorde chain of luxury hotels, it has everything you could want for a sybaritic stay. 🖎 *73 blvd de la Croisette • Map G4 • 04 93 90 12 34 • www.cannesmartinez. grand.hyatt.com • DA • €€€€*

3 J.W. Marriott Cannes, Cannes

Striving to out-do the longer established grand hotels of Cannes, this hotel has outstanding modern facilities and one of the best private beaches. Like its rivals, it attracts a stellar clientele. 🖎 *50 blvd de la Croisette • Map G4 • 04 92 99 70 00 • www. marriott.com • DA • €€€€*

4 Hôtel L'Aiglon, Menton

The Aiglon is set back from the crowded beach and busy traffic of the esplanade and has its own heated swimming pool, surrounded by a semi-tropical garden. It's an easy walk to the sea, but you may not want to leave this oasis. 🖎 *7 ave de la Madone • Map H3 • 04 93 57 55 55 • www. hotelaiglon.net • €€*

5 Le Byblos, St-Tropez

Beloved of rock stars and fashionistas, Le Byblos also has one of St-Trop's trendiest nightspots attached to it. Painted in Art Deco colours worthy of a fashion shoot (for which it is often used), Le Byblos is among the most luxurious hotels in Provence. 🖎 *Ave Paul Signac • Map F5 • 04 94 56 68 00 • Closed Nov–Mar • www. byblos.com • DA • €€€€€*

6 Columbus Monaco, Monaco

This chic hotel aims to mix business with pleasure – its rooms have CD players, Internet access and other high-tech delights. It also has its own private beach, a motorbike taxi service and a fine restaurant. 🖎 *23 ave des Papalins • Map H4 • 00 377 92 05 90 00 • www.columbus hotels.com • DA • €€€€*

7 Monte Carlo Beach Hotel, Roquebrune-Cap-Martin

This 46-room Art Deco showpiece has an Olympic-size pool, a crescent of private beach, three fine restaurants and a general air of exclusive luxury. 🖎 *Ave Princesse-Grace • Map H4 • 04 93 28 66 66 • www.monte-carlo-beach.com • DA • €€€€€*

8 Le Méridien Beach Plaza, Monte Carlo

With a private beach, 2 outdoor pools, 1 indoor pool, a fitness centre, sauna, 2 restaurants and 332 rooms all with private balconies, this is one of the best hotels in Monaco. 🖎 *22 ave Princesse-Grace • Map H4 • 00 377 93 30 98 80 • www.lemeridienmonte carlo.com • DA • €€€€*

9 Hôtel la Baie Dorée, Antibes

With only 17 rooms – all but 2 of which have a view of the sea – this hotel is an alternative to the luxury resorts of the Riviera. There is a private beach and a jetty with loungers set around a tiny harbour. 🖎 *579 blvd de la Garoupe • Map G4 • 04 93 67 30 67 • www. baiedoree.com • €€€€*

10 Résidence de la Pinede, St-Tropez

With its private beach, pool, fine sea views and excellent location, it is hardly surprising that this is a favourite with those who know St-Tropez well. 🖎 *Plage de la Bouillabaisse • Map F5 • 04 94 55 91 00 • Closed mid-Oct–mid-Apr • www.residencepinede. com • DA • €€€€€*

Left **Oustau de la Baumanière, Les-Baux** Right **Riboto de Taven, Les-Baux**

Super Hideaways

1 L'Oustau de Baumanière, Les-Baux-de-Provence

This boutique hotel offers exclusive luxury at a price to match. Suites and rooms are in a complex of beautifully restored old buildings with immaculate garden terraces, a spa and a Michelin-started restaurant. ✆ *Le Val d'Enfer • Map B4 • 04 90 54 33 07 • Closed Dec–Feb • www.oustaudebaumaniere.com • DA • €€€€*

2 Moulin de la Camandoule, Fayence

A swimming pool shaded beneath trees, excellent food, and a delightful location hidden away among vines and pines make this converted olive mill one of the most peaceful and pleasant places to stay. ✆ *Chemin de Notre-Dame-des-Cyprès • Map F4 • 04 94 76 00 84 • www.camandoule.com • No air conditioning • DA • €€*

3 Le Côteau Fleuri, Grimaud

High above the coast on the flanks of the Massif des Maures, on the out-skirts of Grimaud, is this traditional inn, which also serves excellent food. In summertime, meals are served on an exquisitely pretty garden terrace with excellent views. ✆ *Pl des Pénitents • Map F5 • 04 94 43 20 17 • www.coteaufleuri.fr • No air conditioning • €€*

4 La Riboto de Taven, Les-Baux-de-Provence

The "valley of hell" may seem an unlikely location for a romantic hideaway, but the Riboto de Taven, beneath the twisted rocks of the Val d'Enfer, is just that. Great scenery, gardens and a pool add to its appeal. ✆ *Le Val d'Enfer • Map B4 • 04 90 54 34 23 • www.riboto-de-taven.fr • DA • €€€*

5 Le Cagnard, Cagnes-sur-Mer

Only a few minutes' drive from the hurly burly of the Riviera, Le Cagnard is a luxury inn, with lovely rooms in a medieval building, sweeping views and a fine restaurant. All this, and it's located in a pretty village drowning in purple bougainvillea. ✆ *Rue Sous-Barri • Map G4 • 04 93 20 73 22 • www.lecagnard.com • €€€*

6 Grande Bastide, St-Paul-de-Vence

This converted country house just outside St-Paul-de-Vence (though it's too far to walk, save for the most nippy) is calm, friendly and peace-ful, with a pool under palm trees and an immaculately kept garden. Rooms and suites are furnished and decorated in Provençal style, and there are beautiful views. ✆ *Rte de Colle • Map G4 • 04 93 32 50 30 • www.la-grande-bastide.com • No air conditioning • €€€*

7 La Pérouse, Nice

A hidden luxury retreat, La Pérouse has the most outstanding views of Nice's prome-nade. Choose a sea-view room with its own terrace. ✆ *11 quai Rauba Capeu • Map P5 • 04 93 62 34 63 • www.leshotelsduroy.com • €€€€*

8 Hôtel les Deux Rocs, Seillans

Located in a perfectly preserved medieval hill village, this is charming in an old-fashioned way. It has a delightful terrace on a tiny cobbled square, and a restaurant serving the best of Provençal cooking. ✆ *Pl Font d'Amont • Map F4 • 04 94 76 87 32 • www.hoteldeuxrocs.com • No air conditioning • €*

9 Hôtel Villa la Roseraie, Vence

This friendly small hotel has a pool and gardens. Rooms are charming. Ideal for a romantic weekend away at an affordable price. ✆ *128 ave Henri Giraud, rte de Coursegoules • Map G4 • 04 93 58 02 20 • www.villaroseraie.com • No air conditioning • €€*

10 La Ponche, St-Tropez

Stylish, individual and hidden in a tiny square with a view of the fishing port, it's the perfect place to escape town in sum-mer. ✆ *3 rue des Remparts • Map F5 • 04 94 97 02 53 • Closed Nov–mid-Mar • www.laponche.com • €€€€*

Note: *Unless otherwise stated, all hotels accept credit cards, have en suite bathrooms and air conditioning*

Above **Château de la Chèvre d'Or, Eze**

🔟 Château Hotels

1 Château de la Chèvre d'Or, Eze

The wonderful Chèvre d'Or perches high above the sea, looking out over clifftop battlements in this beautifully preserved castle-village. Rooms all have a panoramic view and each one is elegantly decorated with antiques. The hotel has three fine restaurants *(see p102)* and two pools in a pretty setting. ✪ *Rue du Barri • Map H4 • 04 92 10 66 66 • Closed Dec–Feb • www. chevredor.com • €€€€€*

2 Château de la Messardière, St-Tropez

On the outskirts of the village, this seaside palace has a private beach, a luxury spa and a swimming pool and is among the nicest places to stay on this fashionable part of the coast. ✪ *Rte de Tahiti • Map F5 • 04 94 56 76 00, fax 04 94 56 76 01 • www.messardiere.com • DA • €€€€€*

3 Château du Domaine St-Martin, Vence

This palatial hotel in manicured grounds standing on a hilltop site with views of the medieval village and the countryside is one of the most impressive places to stay in Provence. Superb service and excellent food. ✪ *Ave des Templiers • Map G4 • 04 93 58 02 02 • www.chateau-st-martin. com • DA • €€€€€*

4 Château des Alpilles, St-Rémy

The château was built in the 19th century for a prominent Arles family. Standards of service and cuisine rate highly, and the rooms in the castle, the former chapel and converted farmhouses are very cozy. ✪ *Departemental 31 • Map B3 • 04 90 92 03 33 • www.chateaudes alpilles.com • €€€€*

5 Hôtel du Petit Palais, Nice

Surrounded by a large garden with well-established trees, this former palace offers a quiet and scenic retreat away from the bustle of Nice. An elegant but relaxed hotel, it is renowned for its magnificent views of the city and sea. Excellent service. ✪ *17 ave Emile Bieckert • Map P4 • 04 93 62 19 11 • www.petitpalaisnice.com • DA • €€*

6 Château de Taulane, La Martre

An hour's drive from Cannes, this magnificent 18th-century mansion has been transformed into an excellent four-star hotel. It is surrounded by its own estate and an 18-hole, par 72 golf course, considered one of the best in the region. ✪ *Le Domaine du Château de Taulane, Le Logis du Pin • Map G4 • 04 93 40 60 80 • Closed mid-Oct–mid-Apr • www. château-taulane.com • No air conditioning • DA • €€€*

7 Château de Trigance, Trigance

With just 10 rooms this small chateau, built in the 10th century and painstakingly restored by its owners over the last 30 years, is now a three-star hotel with a commendable restaurant. ✪ *Map G4 • 04 94 76 91 18 • Closed Nov–Mar • www. chateau-de-trigance.fr • No air conditioning • €€*

8 Château de Valmer, La Croix Valmer

Surrounded by a 5-ha (12-acre) park with palm trees and a vineyard, this hotel even has its own private beach. ✪ *Map F5 • 04 94 55 15 15 • Closed Oct–Apr • www.chateau valmer.com • No air conditioning • €€€€*

9 Château Eza, Eze

A wonderful collection of medieval buildings now converted into a hotel. Rooms are luxuriously decorated with Oriental rugs and marble bathrooms. ✪ *Rue de la Pise • Map H4 • 04 93 41 12 24 • www. chateaueza.com • €€€€€*

10 La Bastide du Roy René, Aix-en-Provence

Set in stunning grounds, this 15th-century bastide has been beautifully renovated to provide a relaxing environment. ✪ *31 ave des Infirmières • Map D4 • 04 42 37 83 00 • www.citea.com • No air conditioning • DA • €*

Left **Hôtel Splendid, Cannes** Right **Hôtel Les Allées, Cannes**

10 Value-for-Money Hotels

1 Hôtel Splendid, Cannes

Value for money doesn't always mean cheap, but the Splendid, centrally located close to the yacht harbour, is an impressive hotel and is a bargain by Cannes standards. 🔊 *4 rue Félix Faure • Map G4 • 04 97 06 22 22 • www.splendid-hotel-cannes.fr • €€€*

2 Le Windsor, Nice

Exotic Oriental decoration, rooms with frescoed ceilings, a pool surrounded by palm trees and, of all things, an English-style pub, come at an affordable price in this unassuming looking, medium-sized hotel. 🔊 *11 rue Dalpozzo • Map H4 • 04 93 88 59 35 • www.hotelwindsornice.com • €€*

3 Hôtel Les Allées, Cannes

Could this small hotel tucked away in a narrow street not far from the yacht harbour be the best bargain in Cannes? Rooms are simpe but clean and bright (some have balconies with a sea view), with phone, TV and Internet connection, and service is friendly. 🔊 *6 rue Emile-Négrin • Map G4 • 04 93 39 53 90 • www.hotel-des-allees.com • €*

4 Le Benvengudo, Les-Baux-de-Provence

This fine hotel proves that value for money is not all about price: it has comfortable, beautifully decorated rooms (some with terraces), a pool, garden, restaurant and tennis court, all in lovely surroundings. 🔊 *Vallon de l'Arcoule • Map B4 • 04 90 54 32 54 • www.benvengudo.com • €€€*

5 Hôtel Ambassador, Monaco

This budget hotel is right in the heart of Monaco, situated at the foot of the Palais Princier. The rooms are well equipped with a TV, hairdryer and Internet access. The restaurant serves basic Italian cuisine. 🔊 *10 ave Prince-Pierre • Map H5 • 00 377 97 97 96 96 • www.ambassadormonaco.com • €€*

6 Hôtel les Quatre Dauphins, Aix

This small hotel near the centre of Aix has pretty rooms on three floors, with Provençal patterned wallpaper, and modern facilities in the rooms. The service is unfailingly warm and welcoming. 🔊 *54 rue Roux-Alpheran • Map C4 • 04 42 38 16 39 • www.lesquatredauphins.fr • €*

7 Hôtel La Jabotte, Cap d'Antibes

With its clean, bright rooms and chalets and good location, La Jabotte is one of the better bargains in upmarket Antibes. It also has its own car park – quite a rarity. 🔊 *13 ave Max-Maurey • Map G4 • 04 93 61 45 89 • www.jabotte.com • No air conditioning • €€*

8 Hôtel le Richelieu, Marseille

This very affordable hotel on Marseille's waterfront has some rooms with balconies and lovely sea views, a nice breakfast terrace, a ground-floor terraced restaurant, and a pay beach just across the road. 🔊 *52 corniche Kennedy • Map C5 • 04 91 35 78 78 • www.hotel-marseille-richelieu.com • No air conditioning • €*

9 Hôtel Yachting, Marseille

One of the best places to stay in Marseille for the price, this unassuming but friendly, central, 3-star hotel has basic rooms. However, all have a full en suite bathroom. Sound-proofing keeps the street noise to bearable levels. 🔊 *115 rue Paradis • Map C5 • 04 96 10 06 10 • www.hotelyachtingmarseille.com • Visa only • €*

10 Hôtel le Calendal, Arles

A colourful place to stay in a colourful city, the Calendal is brightly decorated and has a very pretty, shady garden café and a comfortable tearoom. Some of the more expensive rooms have terraces and all are air conditioned, making this 3-star hotel a great-value place to stay in generally expensive Arles. 🔊 *5 rue Porte de Laure • Map B4 • 04 90 96 11 89 • www.lecalendal.com • DA • €€*

Note: Unless otherwise stated, all hotels accept credit cards, have en suite bathrooms and air conditioning

Price Categories

For a standard, double room per night (with breakfast if included), taxes and extra charges.

€ under €100
€€ €100–€150
€€€ €150–€250
€€€€ €250–€350
€€€€€ over €350

Above **Camping International, Castellane**

🔟 Under Canvas Choices

1 Camping International

There are numerous camp sites in and around Castellane but this is the best of the bunch. It is close enough to shops and restaurants to be convenient, but far enough away to be untroubled by noise or traffic. The site is surrounded by fields and wooded hills, and the views are terrific. Facilities include a large swimming pool, small supermarket and a friendly, value-for-money restaurant. Cabins are also available. ◈ *Rte Napoléon, Castellane* • *Map F3* • *04 92 83 66 67* • *Closed Oct–Mar* • *www. camping-international.fr* • *€*

2 Camping des Oliviers

This small camp site amid olive trees on a hillside is within easy reach of Cannes and Antibes but is in a very quiet location. It has a simple snack restaurant and bar, but the main attraction is the swimming pool, on a terrace with panoramic views. ◈ *274 Chemin des Hautes Vignasses, Biot* • *Map G4* • *04 93 65 02 79* • *Closed Oct–Apr* • *No credit cards* • *€*

3 Camping Antipolis

The best thing about this enormous, 4-star full-service camp site is its location: just outside Antibes, minutes' walk from the sea and with a local railway station with frequent connections into Cannes. An excellent choice for families. ◈ *Ave du Pylone, La Brague, Antibes* • *Map G4* • *04 93 33 93 99* • *Closed Oct–Feb* • *www.camping-antipolis. com* • *DA* • *€*

4 Les Cigales

Billing itself as an "open-air hotel", this camp site just west of Cannes has spaces for tents and caravans under the olive trees, cabins and mobile homes to rent, and a pool with a toddlers' lagoon. The site is on a river with boats, kayaks and pedalos to rent. ◈ *505 ave de la Mer, Mandelieu La Napoule* • *Map G4* • *04 93 49 23 53* • *www.lescigales.com* • *€*

5 Camping la Pinède

A cheap and cheerful alternative to St-Tropez's hotels – with facilities that include a mini-golf course, children's play area, restaurant and snack bar. ◈ *RD 14, Grimaud* • *Map F5* • *04 94 56 04 36* • *www.lapinede-camping.com* • *Closed Nov–Mar* • *DA* • *€*

6 Camping Abri de Camargue

This clean, medium-sized camp site is near a sandy beach. It has an indoor and outdoor pool, a play area, its own cinema, bar, shop and restaurant, and *pétanque* (boules) and tennis courts nearby. ◈ *320 Rte du Phare de l'Espiguette, Le Grau du Roi* • *Map B4* • *04 66 51 54 83* • *Closed Oct–Mar* • *www. abridecamargue.com* • *€*

7 Le Rossignol

A 3-star camp site with a pool, spaces for tents and motorhomes, and 4-person bungalows. ◈ *2074 ave Jean-Michard-Pelissier, Antibes* • *Map G4* • *04 93 33 56 98* • *Closed Oct–Mar* • *www.camping rossignol.com* • *DA* • *€*

8 La Merio

This small 1-star site with space for 40 tents is in the heart of the Parc National du Mercantour (see p40). Not luxurious, but it does offer hot showers. ◈ *1344 Rte de la Colmiane, St-Martin-Vesubie* • *Map G2* • *04 93 03 30 38* • *Closed Oct–May* • *www. saintmartinvesubie.fr* • *No credit cards* • *€*

9 Camping le Pesquier

This 2-star site has a small pool, and tents are pitched under shady trees. ◈ *RN 85 Route de Digne-les-Bains, Castellane* • *Map F3* • *04 92 83 66 81* • *Closed Oct–Mar* • *www.camping-le-pesquier.com* • *DA* • *€*

10 Camping les Romarins

While spartan, this 2-star site is worth it for the views along the coast. There is a snack-restaurant and bar. ◈ *Grande Corniche, D2564, Eze* • *Map F3* • *04 93 01 81 64* • *Closed Oct–Mar* • *€*

Left and right **Le Gîte de Chasteuil**

Gîtes and Chambres d'Hôte

1 Le Hameau de Pichovet

Situated near the lavender fields of Luberon National Park, this stone house offers four guest rooms and two apartments. The pool is heated from mid-May to mid-October, and the restaurant provides authentic dishes at a family-style dining table or on the terrace. ⊛ *Campagne Pichovet, Vachères • Map D3 • 04 92 73 33 48 • www.hameau-de-pichovet.com • No air conditioning • €€*

2 Le Gîte de Chasteuil

This delightful bed-and-breakfast is high on a hillside in a tiny hamlet close to the east end of the Canyon du Verdon, with mountain views. For walkers, the GR4 long-distance footpath passes right through the village. Each bedroom has its own bathroom, and one has a kitchenette. ⊛ *Hameau de Chasteuil, Castellane • Map F3 • 04 92 83 72 45 • www.gitedechasteuil.com • No credit cards • No air conditioning • €*

3 Leï Souco

Near to some famous beaches, this lovely stone house is surrounded by 10 ha (25 acres) planted with mimosa, olives and eucalyptus. Chambres d'hôtes and studios. ⊛ *Plaine de Camarat, Ramatuelle • Map F5 • 04 94 79 80 22 • www.leisouco.com • No air conditioning • €€*

4 Le Mas de la Beaume

Throw open the windows and look out onto the Alpilles mountains or the château de Gordes from this delightful old farmhouse. The three rooms and two suites are individually decorated and furnished with quirky antiques and fine linens. The swimming pool is hidden in an olive grove, and breakfast comes with home-made jams. ⊛ *Gordes-Village • Map C3 • 04 90 72 02 96 • www. labeaume.com • No air conditioning • €€*

5 La Vieille Bastide

This lovely farmhouse has four bedrooms, and is set in an estate where tortoises roam and lavender, fruit trees and olives grow. It has two pools, a luxury kitchen and is within walking distance of the village. ⊛ *La Garde Freinet, Golfe de St-Tropez • Map F5 • 04 94 60 00 59 • www. ownersdirect.co.uk • No en suite bathrooms • No air conditioning • €€€*

6 La Prévôté

"A well-kept secret amongst friends" is the motto of this B&B, set in a former monastery. Rooms are spacious and stylish, and the gourmet restaurant uses only fresh, local produce. ⊛ *4 rue Jean-Jacques Rousseau, l'Isle-sur-la-Sorgue • Map C3 • 04 90 38 57 29 • www. la-prevote.fr • No air conditioning • €€€*

7 La Grand Barthelière

This grand 18th-century bastide with lovely grounds and a large pool was completely renovated in 2013. ⊛ *Route de Cavaillon • Map B4 • 04 90 78 99 72 • www.bartheliere. com • Closed Dec–Mar • No air conditioning • €€*

8 Le Mas de l'Esparou

This small guesthouse has views of the castle and the Alpilles mountains. The building is set in pine woods, and each of the four rooms has its own terrace. ⊛ *Rte de St-Rémy, 13520 Les-Baux-de-Provence • Map B4 • 04 90 54 41 32 • www.lesparou-lesbaux. com • No credit cards • No air conditioning • €*

9 La Bastide Rose

This pretty farmhouse among vineyards and orchards offers three apartments, two gîtes, two chambres d'hôtes and a pool. Each room has its own kitchenette and terrace. ⊛ *Quartier du Gaudran, Salernes • Map B4 • 04 94 70 63 30 • www. bastide-rose.com • No credit cards • €*

10 La Garance en Provence

This restored 17th-century farmhouse has five comfy bedrooms and a pool. ⊛ *4010 rte de St-Saturin d'Avignon, Le Thor • Map B4 • 04 90 33 72 78 • www. garance-provence.com • No air conditioning • €€€*

Note: Unless otherwise stated, all hotels accept credit cards, have en suite bathrooms and air conditioning

Price Categories

For a standard, double room per night (with breakfast if included), taxes and extra charges.

€	under €100
€€	€100–€150
€€€	€150–€250
€€€€	€250–€350
€€€€€	over €350

Above Hôtel de Paris

🔟 Health and Beauty Spas

Mercure Thalassa
This 105-room hotel stands next to a fine sandy beach, with views of a yacht marina and the pretty port of Fréjus. It specializes in using the beneficial effects of the marine environment, including sea water, seaweed, sand and other substances, together with the Mediterranean climate. 🔍 *Port-Fréjus Ouest, Fréjus • Map F4 • 04 94 52 55 00 or 08 25 82 55 28 • www.thalassa. com • DA • €€*

Hôtel le Couvent des Minimes
This beautiful former convent boasts the first L'Occitane hotel spa, along with a pool, an aromatic garden and a selection of restaurants and bars. Relax in 1 of the 40 rooms or 6 suites. 🔍 *Chemin des Jeux de Maï, Mane • Map D3 • 04 92 74 77 77 • www. couventdesminimes-hotelspa.com • €€€*

Hôtel Aquabella
The Romans were among the first to revere the healing properties of the thermal springs of Mont Ste-Victoire, where you can take the waters in a modernized 18th-century palace, with an array of power showers, hydro-massage and mud wraps to eliminate stress and toxins. 🔍 *2 rue des Etuves, Aix-en-Provence • Map C4 • 04 42 99 15 00 • www.hotelaix.fr • €€*

Hôtel Grande Avignon
Just outside Avignon, the 4-star hotel is a complex of 30 junior suites, each with whirlpool bath. There are also 18- and 9-hole golf courses nearby. 🔍 *22 chemin de la Blanchère, Vedène • Map B3 • 04 90 02 09 09 • www.residhotel. com • DA • €€€*

Hôtel le Méridien
On the ninth floor of one of Nice's finest hotels, the beauty and fitness centre offers everything from sauna and massage to manicure and make-up advice. 🔍 *1 Promenade des Anglais, Nice • Map G4 • 04 97 03 44 44 • www.lemeri diennice.com • DA • €€€€*

Hôtel du Grand Paris
Right in the centre of the thermal resort of Digne, this luxurious hotel offers a range of treatments in the adjoining hot springs, which are used to treat arthritis, rheumatism and respiratory conditions. 🔍 *19 blvd Thiers, Digne-les-Bains • Map E2 • 04 92 31 11 15 • www.hotel-grand-paris.com • €€*

Le Mas de la Cremaillère
A range of spa packages at the sulphur-rich thermal springs of Gréoux-les-Bains is available to guests in this farmhouse-hotel with swimming pool, golf practice range and a restaurant noted for its Provençal menu. 🔍 *Rte de Riez, Gréoux-les-Bains • Map E2 • 04 92 70 40 04 • Closed mid-Dec–Mar • www.mascremaillere greoux.com • €€*

Villa Borghese
A modern hotel close to Gréoux's famous hot springs, the Borghese offers a range of menus to complement the health and beauty treatments available at the spa. Other facilities include a sauna, swimming pool and solarium. 🔍 *Ave des Thermes, Gréoux-les-Bains • Map E2 • 04 92 78 00 91 • Closed Dec–Feb • www.hotel-villaborghese.com • €€€*

Hôtel de Paris
Monte Carlo's most glamorous hotel has direct access to the most modern health spa in Europe. The hotel has four restaurants, its own hairdresser and luxury boutiques. 🔍 *Pl du Casino, Monte Carlo • Map H3 • 00 377 98 06 30 00 • www. montecarloresort.com • DA • €€€€€*

Le Mas de Pierre
Located in the beautiful countryside outside of St-Paul-de-Vence, this luxurious 4-star hotel has been designed to help you relax. Details include a rose garden with stunning views, a *hammam* and a heated pool. 🔍 *2320 rte des Serres, St-Paul-de-Vence • Map G4 • 04 93 59 00 10 • www.lemasdepierre. com • DA • €€€€€*

General Index

Index

Index

Acknowledgments

Main contributors

Robin Gauldie is a travel journalist who has visited Provence regularly since 1972 and divides his time between London and the South of France. After several years working for *Travel Trade Gazette*, Robin is now a freelance journalist and author of more than a dozen guidebooks to destinations ranging from Greece to Goa.

Lancashire-born Anthony Peregrine lives in the Languedoc region of southern France, and works as an author and journalist specializing in food, wine and travel. His work has appeared in the *Daily Telegraph*, *Daily Mail* and on BBC Radio 4.

Produced by Sargasso Media Ltd, London

Project Editor Zoë Ross
Designer Stephen Woosnam-Savage
Picture Research Monica Allende
Proofreader Stewart J Wild
Editorial Assistance Sophie Warne

Main Photographer Demetrio Carrasco

Additional Photography Max Alexander, Robin Gauldie, John Heseltine, Rough Guides/Michelle Grant, Kim Sayer, Alan Williams

Illustrator Chris Orr & Associates

FOR DORLING KINDERSLEY
Senior Art Editor Marisa Renzullo
Senior Publishing Manager Louise Lang

Publishing Managers Kate Poole, Helen Townsend
Art Director Gillian Allan
Cartography Co-ordinator Casper Morris
DTP Jason Little
Revisions Team Nicola Erdpresser, Emer FitzGerald, Lisa Fox-Mullen, Fay Franklin, Michelle Arness Frederic, Anna Freiberger, Rhiannon Furbear, Laura Jones, Bharti Karakoti, Priya Kukadia, Delphine Lawrance, Hayley Maher, Catherine Palmi, Lyn Parry, Susie Peachey, Ellen Root, Sands Publishing Solutions, Catherine Skipper, Conrad Van Dyk, Karen Villabona, Dora Whitaker
Production Joanna Bull, Marie Ingledew

Maps James Anderson

Special Assistance

The authors would like to thank Ann Noon, Maison de la France, London; Sybil Darrington, Monaco Visitor and Convention Bureau; Sandra Jurinic, Office de Tourisme et des Congrès, Nice; Yvonne Perettoni, Office de Tourisme, Marseille; Danielle Damiani, Comité Départemental de Tourisme, Vaucluse; Hoverspeed

Picture Credits

a - above; b - below/bottom; c - centre; f - far; l - left; r - right; t - top.

Works of art have been reproduced with the permission of the following copyright holders:

©ADAGP, Paris and DACS, London 2011 34tl, 104tl, 105t; © Succession H. Matisse/DACS,

London 2011 32tl; © Succession Picasso/DACS. London 2011 93t.

The publishers would like to thank the following individuals, companies, and picture libraries for permission to reproduce their photographs:

HOSTELLERIE DE L'ABBAYE DE LA CELLE: 85tl; AISA, Barcelona: 7tr, 7c, 12b, 20-21c, 24-25c; AKG, London: 34tr, 37r, © ADAGP, Paris/DACS, London 2011 *Manteau de porte* Maillol 34b, © ADAGP, Paris/Dacs, London 2011 *Sailing boats in the harbour of St Tropez* Paul Signac 35r, © ADAGP, Paris and DACS, London 2011 *Jetée d'Honfleur* Raoul Dufy 36tl, © Succession Picasso/DACS 2011 *Self-Portrait* Picasso 36tr, *La Montagne Sainte-Victoire, vue de Bibemus* Cézanne 36b, *Lilac Bush*, Vincent van Gogh 37t, Cameraphoto Epoche 29t, Erich Lessing 29r, Lothar Peter 35t; ALAMY IMAGES: Pixonnet.com/Goran Strandsten 139tl; AVIGNON TOURISME: Clémence Rodde 9bl.

BASTIDE DE CAPELONGUE: 125tl.

CEPHAS: Mick Rock 52tl, 52tr, 52b, 53r; CORBIS: 6cl, 56b, 57r, 58t, 58b, 59c, 59r.

DREAMSTIME.COM: Anshar 86tr; Arsty 96-7; Gianliguori 80-1; Venakr 4-5; Wastesoul 62-3

FAIENCERIE FIGUERES: 68tl.

GETTY IMAGES: Peter Adams 133tl; Hemis/Franck Guiziou 113cl; GITES DE FRANCE: 132tl.

WWW.HOTEL–MARTINEZ.COM: 50tl; HOTEL RESTAURANT LES DEUX FRERES: 103tl.

LEONARDO MEDIABANK: 50br.

MA NOLAN'S IRISH PUB: 90tl; MONTE-CARLO S.B.M. HOTELS AND CASINOS: 140tr.

NICE TOURISM: 135tl.

RESTAURANT LE GARAGE: 75TL.

STA TRAVEL GROUP: 135 tr.

All other images are ©DK for further information see www.dkimages.com

Acknowledgments